THE
CAMBRIDGE
ARMORIAL

THE CAMBRIDGE ARMORIAL

compiled by members of
THE CAMBRIDGE UNIVERSITY HERALDIC AND
GENEALOGICAL SOCIETY

edited by
Cecil Humphery-Smith
Heather E. Peek
Gordon H. Wright
and the late
C.W. Scott-Giles,
Fitzalan Pursuivant of Arms Extraordinary
who wrote the Introduction and prepared
many of the illustrations

with a Foreword by the late
Earl Mountbatten of Burma

ORBIS · LONDON

First published in Great Britain by Orbis Publishing Limited, London, 1985

This volume has been produced in association with Tabard Publications

Printed in Great Britain by Netherwood Dalton & Co Ltd, Huddersfield

ISBN 0-85613-871-1

CONTENTS

FOREWORD BY EARL
MOUNTBATTEN OF BURMA 6

PREFACE 7

INTRODUCTION 8

THE CITY OF CAMBRIDGE 14

THE UNIVERSITY OF
CAMBRIDGE 18

THE REGIUS PROFESSORS 22

PETERHOUSE 30

CLARE COLLEGE 34

PEMBROKE COLLEGE 38

GONVILLE AND CAIUS
COLLEGE 42

TRINITY HALL 46

CORPUS CHRISTI COLLEGE 50

KING'S COLLEGE 54

QUEENS' COLLEGE 58

ST CATHARINE'S COLLEGE 64

JESUS COLLEGE 68

CHRIST'S COLLEGE AND
ST JOHN'S COLLEGE 72

MAGDALENE COLLEGE 76

TRINITY COLLEGE 80

EMMANUEL COLLEGE 84

SIDNEY SUSSEX COLLEGE 88

DOWNING COLLEGE 92

GIRTON COLLEGE 96

NEWNHAM COLLEGE 100

SELWYN COLLEGE 104

FITZWILLIAM COLLEGE 108

CHURCHILL COLLEGE 112

NEW HALL 116

DARWIN COLLEGE 118

WOLFSON COLLEGE 120

CLARE HALL 122

HUGHES HALL 123

ST EDMUND'S HOUSE 124

LUCY CAVENDISH COLLEGE 126

HOMERTON COLLEGE 128

ROBINSON COLLEGE 130

RIDLEY HALL 131

WESTCOTT HOUSE 134

THE WESTMINSTER AND
CHESHUNT COLLEGES 135

WESLEY HOUSE 138

THE PERSE SCHOOL 139

THE LEYS SCHOOL 141

GLOSSARY 142

FOREWORD

It is remarkable that undergraduates can achieve any major work through a University Society during the few hard years that they spend at study and, of course, generations of students pass by and continuity of interest in such Societies is an ever-present problem.

Through the encouragement and devotion of Mr Wilfrid Scott-Giles, Fitzalan Pursuivant Extraordinary, of Sidney Sussex College, the Cambridge University Heraldic and Genealogical Society have, in some four generations of undergraduates, produced a signal and colourful contribution to the study of the history and heraldry of their colleges.

Heraldry so often reflects the genealogical stories associated with the foundations of such institutions and this is well illustrated in this book.

Mountbatten of Burma
A.F.

Admiral of the Fleet
the Earl Mountbatten of Burma
(1900–1979)

PREFACE

As long ago as 1961 plans were drawn up by the Cambridge University Heraldic and Genealogical Society to compile a record of the armorial bearings of the University and colleges, with notes on the origins, historical associations and heraldic significance of the arms. A number of members of the Society undertook to collect information from college records and other authentic sources, and in some cases two or three had a hand in compiling notes on the heraldry of a particular college. In the process of gathering material, it was seen to be desirable to extend the scope of the book so as to include the heraldry of the City and of certain colleges and schools external to the University. The material assembled by members has been subject to sufficient revision to ensure uniformity in the plan and scope of the various articles, and one of the members responsible for this editorship has also written the Introduction.

The following members have contributed to the making of this volume:

R.M. Ball (Peterhouse)   P.R. Cowell (Gonville and Caius)
J.M. Daly (Pembroke)   W.M.T. Fowle (Clare)   P.J. Gooderson (Queens')
J.D.U. Green (Queens')   E.J.M. Hepper (Pembroke)
N.A. Hooton (Selwyn)   M.S. Howe (Trinity)   A.P. Masters (King's)
C.R.J. Humphery-Smith (a Vice-President; St John's)
D.C. Moss (Magdalene)   C. Mellor (Hon. Fellow, The Heraldry Society)
C.P.L. Openshaw (St Catharine's)   Miss Heather E. Peek (a Vice-President; formerly Keeper of the University Archives; Wolfson and Girton)
S.J. Pimlott (Sidney Sussex)   C.W. Scott-Giles (Sidney Sussex; *obiit* 1982)
T.C. Stancliffe (Trinity)   D. Thorpe (St John's)   J.H. Vie (Downing)
R.H. Wildman (Clare)   G.H. Wright (Senior Treasurer; Clare and King's).

Special thanks are due to the late Prof. G.W.H. Lampe, Dr J.D. Pickles, the late Prof. D. Winton Thomas, and many others, for help on particular points. John Bainbridge and Thomas Meek have helped enormously with the artwork preparation and several original drawings.

INTRODUCTION

Cambridge is rich in heraldry. Arms are borne not only by the City and the University but also by all of the thirty-one colleges and by some other institutions situated in Cambridge but not forming part of the University.

Of the seventeen ancient colleges a few received formal grants of arms at or shortly after their foundation. Others acquired their heraldic emblems in the first instance by using the armorial insignia associated with their founders. These devices are found displayed on their buildings, and sometimes as part of their corporate seals. Long after the lifetimes of the founders, arms so used came to be identified with the foundations and were eventually recorded as the arms of the colleges, or granted to them with some appropriate difference, by the heraldic authorities.

The earliest record of the arms used by the colleges is a page of drawings in the *Catalogus Cancellariorum etc.* which forms an appendix to Archbishop Matthew Parker's *De Antiquitate Britannicae Ecclesiae* (1572), of which some copies contain a corrected sheet of drawings apparently made in 1573. Paintings of the arms of the University and colleges in Robert Hare's *Transcripts of the Privileges of the University of Cambridge* (1587) in the University Archives (UA Hare A. vol. 1) closely follow Parker's record and do not include changes made in the arms of some colleges in 1575. Another source of information is John Hammond's map of Cambridge (1592), in the Bodleian Library, Oxford, which shows the arms of the colleges in the margin.

The only previous book on the subject is *The Arms of the University and Colleges of Cambridge* by R.W. Oldfield (A. & C. Black Ltd, 1931). Since its publication there have been some revisions of the arms of the older colleges and grants to most colleges founded after that date, as well as fresh information deriving from subsequent research.

Parker's record of 1572 shows that seven colleges were then using the undifferenced arms of their founders, namely Clare, Pembroke, Trinity Hall, Jesus, Christ's, St John's, and Magdalene, while Gonville and Caius bore the arms of its two founders impaled, i.e. side by side on one shield. Peterhouse is given St Peter's keys in 1572 and its founder's personal arms in the corrected sheet of 1573. To Queens' Parker attributes as arms the device on a seal given to the college by Richard III – a cross and crosier saltirewise★ surmounted by a boar's head – but an earlier seal bore the arms of Queen Margaret of Anjou, and these are given as the college arms on Hammond's map.

Before 1570 only two colleges received grants of arms distinct from those of their founders, namely King's in 1448 and Trinity probably at its foundation, although in this case no patent can be found.

In 1570, at the request of Archbishop Parker, Robert Cooke, Clarenceux King of Arms, granted arms to Corpus Christi College to replace a device of a religious character which dated from the foundation of the college but which came to be regarded as superstitious after the Reformation. This was the first of a series of grants and confirmations by Cooke which resulted in the University, the Regius Professors and most of the colleges bearing authorised arms. He also confirmed arms to the Borough (now City) of Cambridge with a grant of crest and supporters.

It is fitting that the development of Cambridge heraldry should owe so much to Robert Cooke, since he was a Master of Arts of the University, a member of St John's College, and the first known Cambridge graduate to become a King of Arms. He was appointed Chester Herald in 1562 and Clarenceux in 1567, and in the latter capacity his province, covering all England south of the River Trent, included Cambridgeshire.

In Parker's *Catalogus* (1572) the University was represented by a shield bearing a device on its seal. This showed the figure of the Chancellor seated between two doctors on a bridge over water. This single instance of a seal-

★ See the Glossary on page 142 for heraldic terms.   9

device given shield form did not establish it as armorial bearings, but it indicated that the University felt the need to possess arms, and in 1573 Robert Cooke satisfied this by granting the noble coat which appeared in the corrected page of the *Catalogus* and has since been borne by the University.

In 1575 Cooke made a Visitation of Cambridgeshire and reviewed the arms used by most of the Cambridge colleges, although some did not appear before him, perhaps because his summons was not so compelling for corporate bodies as for individuals. In the case of the University and of King's and Corpus Christi he had only to record the arms which had already been formally granted, while he confirmed the arms used by Trinity College, thereby implying that he was satisfied there was authority for them. He also confirmed the right of Clare to bear the arms of its foundress without difference, probably because there was evidence that this was the Lady Clare's own wish. Cooke did not deal with Pembroke, but at the Visitation of 1684 this college also was allowed the undifferenced arms of its foundress.

With regard to other colleges using their founders' arms, Cooke thought it necessary to add a border to the shield so as to create distinctive arms for the college while preserving those of the founder as the central feature. In the shield of Queens' he surrounded the six quarterings of Queen Margaret of Anjou with a green border. Peterhouse and Jesus, each founded by a bishop of Ely, were given their founders' coats within a red border charged with gold crowns from the arms of the see. The impaled coats of Edmund Gonville and John Caius were given to their foundation within a border compony argent and sable. The arms of Bishop Bateman, founder of Trinity Hall, consisted of an ermine crescent on black within a silver engrailed border, and these were differenced for the college by making the border a plain one of ermine.

St Catharine's was not included in Cooke's review but the Catherine wheel, from its seal, was allowed as the arms of the college at the 1684 Visitation.

The arms used by Christ's, St John's and Magdalene were not recorded at either Cooke's Visitation or that of 1684. Christ's and St John's, both founded by the Lady Margaret Beaufort, are credited with her arms in Parker's *Catalogus*, Hare's *Transcripts* and Hammond's map, while in the same records Magdalene is given the arms of its founder, Lord Audley of Walden. The founders' arms are also attributed to these colleges in certain books and manuscripts at the College of Arms, but not in any document there regarded as an authoritative record. The position therefore appears to be that, while these colleges have long used their founders' arms as their own, their right to do so has never been established with the Kings of Arms.

Robert Cooke granted arms to Emmanuel College in 1588. Apparently misled by a genealogical claim now regarded as suspect, he allowed the founder, Sir Walter Mildmay, three blue lions on silver purporting to be the ancient arms of Mildmay, and one such lion became the principal charge in the arms granted to the college.

Finally in 1590, at the request of Dr Thomas Lorkin, 'Publicke Reader of the King's Physicke Lecture', Cooke granted arms of office to the Readers, or Regius Professors, of Physic (or Medicine), Law, Divinity, Hebrew and Greek.

Sidney Sussex College missed Cooke's attention, being founded two years after his death. From the first it used the arms of its foundress – the coat of Radcliffe Earl of Sussex impaling that of Sidney – and while there is a record that these were granted to the college in 1675, no patent can be found. Downing College was granted the arms of its founder with the addition of a border charged with roses.

Grants of arms have been obtained by all of the later foundations, except for St Edmund's House.

This record lists constituent colleges in the order in which they were recognised by the University and includes some foundations situated in Cambridge but not officially connected with the University. Among these are Wesley House and Ridley Hall which have obtained grants of arms; Westcott House, which displays the arms of Bishop Westcott; Westminster College, which has a device long associated with a branch of the Presbyterian Church; and Cheshunt (now associated with Westminster) which uses the arms of its foundress, the Countess of Huntingdon. The Perse School and the Leys School are also included. Addenbrooke's Hospital uses the arms of John Addenbrooke, sometime fellow and bursar of St Catharine's; Fisher House, the arms of Bishop Fisher of Rochester; and the Cambridge College of Arts and Technology a device of its own.

We should be failing in our duty if we were to omit mention of 'Bull College', so named by the Provost of King's in October 1945 on the arrival of 145 American officers and men at the Red Cross centre at the Bull Hotel in Trumpington Street. They used a device to be sewn on the men's tunics consisting of the University arms with a chief of the flag of the United States impaling a bull's head caboshed with in chief the Union Jack and enty in base of the U.S. Army badge!

The shields of Selwyn College and Ridley Hall provide instances of the long-standing practice among bishops of impaling the arms of their see with their personal arms – the arms of the see being placed on the dexter side and the bishop's personal coat on the sinister. This practice was followed by some other dignitaries including heads of colleges in the universities, and in Cambridge there are many instances of college arms impaled with those of the Master, Provost or President. The five Regius Professors possessing official coats of arms may bear these either alone or impaled with their personal coats.

A man holding two offices to which arms appertain may marshal both coats with his personal arms. For instance, in King's College chapel the monument, dated 1651, to Samuel Collins, Provost of King's and Regius Professor of Divinity, has a cartouche bearing in the upper part the arms of the college and the professorship side by side, and in the base the griffin of Collins. In Trinity Hall chapel ceiling, dating from 1730, there is a shield commemorating Stephen Gardiner (d. 1555), sometime Master of Trinity Hall and Bishop of Winchester. Here the shield is divided vertically into three, the coat of Gardiner being placed in the centre between that of the See of Winchester on the dexter and the college on the sinister side. The shield is encircled by the Garter, the Bishop of Winchester being Prelate of that Order.

Occasionally three official coats are found marshalled with a personal one. At St Catharine's College there is a painting of Dr John Gostlin (1566–1625), who was at one time Master of Gonville and Caius, Regius Professor of Physic and Vice-Chancellor of the University. The painting includes a shield in which his personal and official coats are quartered, *viz*: (1) Gostlin, (2) the Professorship of Physic, (3) the University, (4) Gonville and Caius (for the college, but without the border).

For the City of Cambridge the full achievement of arms is shown, comprising shield, helm with mantling, crest and supporters. The armorial bearings of the University and most of the older colleges consist only of a shield of arms, possibly for the good reason that a corporate body cannot wear a helmet and crest. In the case of the Regius Professors and those colleges which have been granted crests, these are shown on a crest-wreath above the shield but not placed on a helm – a permissible practice adopted here to give prominence to the essential heraldic features and to avoid occupying space with repetitive helms and mantling. In every case the helm would be of the type appropriate to an esquire – a closed helm in profile facing to the dexter. In addition to arms and crests, Selwyn and Darwin have obtained badges, and these are illustrated below the shields.

By reference to the illustrations, readers unfamiliar with heraldic terms should be able to follow the verbal descriptions (blazons) of armorial bearings. Where of special interest the blazon from the original grant has been quoted. There is also a glossary at the end of this book.

The arms of the City, the University and the colleges may be used for official purposes on seals, documents and publications, and decoratively on buildings, furniture, plate and other property. They may also be displayed in the form of banners, and when the flags fly over Cambridge on days of national or local celebration the variety of heraldic banners adds interest to the gaiety of bunting.

THE CITY OF CAMBRIDGE

Arms

As blazoned in the grant of 1575: Gules a bridge, in chief a flower de luce [*sic*, for lis], gold between two roses silver, on a poynt wave three botes sables.

Crest

Upon a wreath gold and gules, on a mounte vert a bridge silver; mantled gules doubled silver.

Supporters

Two Neptune's horses, the upper part gules, the nether part proper fyned gold.

The painting on the patent supplies details not given in the blazon. The bridge in the arms, gold, is of one arch surmounted by three towers, while the one forming the crest is silver and has two arches and a castle-like superstructure with three domed towers and two small turrets between them. A 'point wavy' means that the part of the shield below the bridge is treated to represent water – frequently shown as *barry wavy argent and azure* in later versions of the arms. The black boats have each one mast with a yard-arm and furled sail.

The grant by Robert Cooke, Clarenceux King of Arms, in 1575, added the crest and supporters to what were described as the 'auncient armes' of the town and borough (now city). However, this does not imply that the shield of arms was in use before that date. Cooke's reference to ancient arms was probably to the device on the former Corporation seal, which consisted of a bridge of four arches over water, and above it the Royal Arms, *Quarterly France Modern and England*, supported by two angels. In devising the arms,

Cooke followed the design on the seal to the extent of retaining a bridge over water as the central feature and placing above it royal emblems – the fleur-de-lis and roses – instead of the Royal Arms, seldom used in civic heraldry.

Cambridge began and grew where ancient highways converged to cross a river at its highest navigable point. It is therefore fitting that a bridge and boats should be the principal emblems in the arms, and that the shield should be supported by heraldic sea-horses. On the rising ground to the north of the Great Bridge (now Magdalene Bridge) a castle was built on the orders of William I. This still existed when the arms were granted, and it is probable that the towers on the bridge in the shield, and the castellated structure forming the crest, represent the commanding proximity of Cambridge castle to the Great Bridge. In the crest the bridge is shown with water under the arches, but set on a green mount, which may be intended for the motte which was a prominent feature of the hill above the bridge, and still exists.

THE UNIVERSITY OF CAMBRIDGE

Arms
Gules, a cross ermine between four lions passant gardant or, and on the cross a closed book fessways gules clasped and garnished gold, the clasps downward.

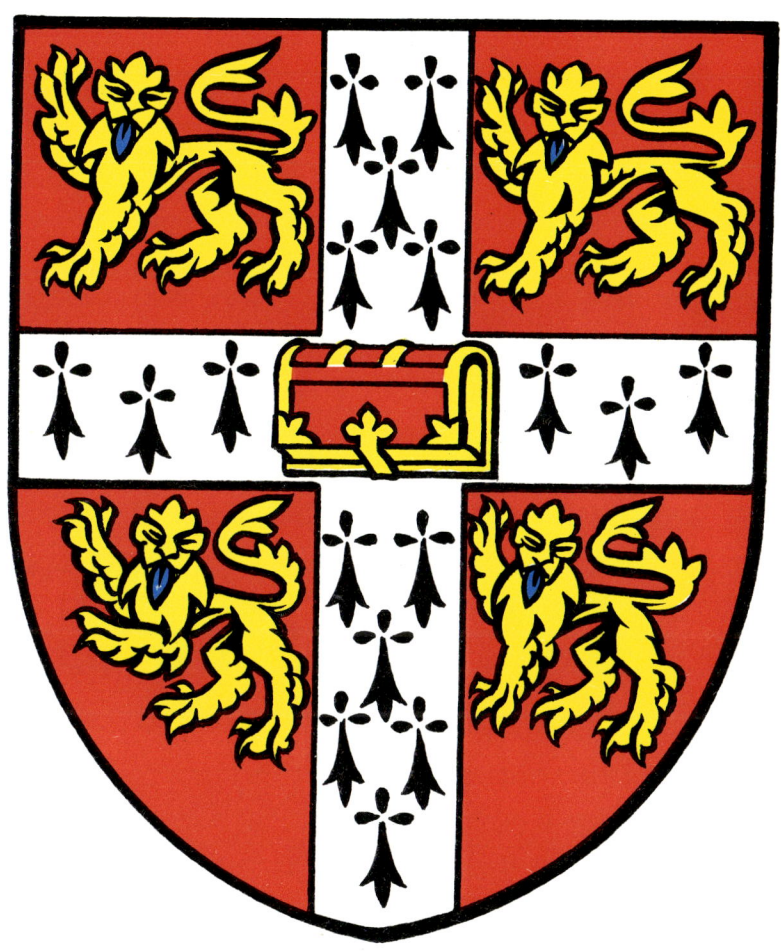

These arms were granted in 1573 by Robert Cooke, Clarenceux King of Arms, to Sir William Cecil, K.G., Lord Burghley, Chancellor of the University, and to the members and scholars of the University and their successors. In the patent the arms are blazoned: *Gules sur ung croix dermines entre quatre Lions passant d'or ung Livre de gules.*

This blazon is imprecise, and it is necessary to refer to the painting on the patent for the fact that the lions passant are also gardant, and for the position and details of the book.

The seal of the University in use before the arms were granted depicted the Chancellor seated between two standing figures in academical dress, all on a bridge of three arches over water containing fishes. In Archbishop Parker's *Catalogus* (1572) this design was shown on a shield and described as the arms of the University. This single instance of the use of the seal device in this way did not establish it as armorial bearings. However, it shows that at that time the University authorities needed to possess arms. Clarenceux Cooke, himself a graduate of the University, met the need by granting them arms in the following year. In 1580 a new seal was made, in which the Chancellor and the other two figures were retained, but the bridge below them was replaced by a shield bearing the arms of the University.

In a record of the arms of bodies represented at the Council of Constance in 1414, the two English universities were represented by the Royal Arms (*Quarterly France Modern and England*) with the addition of a book gules. For Cambridge, the book was shown with its back to the sinister, while for Oxford it was the other way round. It is probable that Clarenceux Cooke had this in mind when he devised arms for Cambridge, since he included the lions of England and a red book in his design.

The letters patent granting arms to the University (preserved in the Archives) are in Latin except for the French blazon of the arms. They are signed 'Robĩs Cooke Alias Clarencieulx' and it is possible that the rest of the document is in his hand. An entry in the University Audit Book for the year 1574–5 shows that the fees payable in connection with the grant amounted to £3 6s. 8d. Today they would be about £1000.

Unfortunately for the historical aspect of the patent, Cooke's enthusiasm in granting arms to his own University led him to enter into controversy as to whether Cambridge or Oxford is the older, and he supported the claim of Cambridge by stating that it was founded by Cantaber in 394 B.C.

While the arms were new Cooke's omission of the term *gardant* from the description of the lions gave rise to error by those who had the blazon but not the illustration before them. For instance, in the Fitzwilliam Museum there is a late sixteenth-century book with the University arms stamped on the cover, with the lions shown as passant, looking ahead, not as gardant, with their heads turned to face the viewer. A corrected form of the same stamp, showing the lions passant gardant, appears on some books of a slightly later date.

THE REGIUS PROFESSORS

In 1590, at the request and expense of Dr Thomas Lorkin, 'Publicke Reader of the King's Phisicke lecture' in the University, Robert Cooke, Clarenceux King of Arms, granted arms of office and crests to be borne by the five Public Readers or Regius Professors at that time – namely of Physic, Law, Divinity, Hebrew and Greek – and by their successors. These professorships were founded by Henry VIII in 1540. Public reader and professor were at that time alternative descriptions, although today a professor is senior to a reader.

While holding one of these appointments a professor may use the appropriate arms and crest, and if he also has personal arms he may impale his official and personal coats, the former being placed in the dexter half of the shield. The crest-wreath or torse, forming the base for the crest, is of the heraldic tinctures predominant in the relevant shield, but in every case the mantling, when shown, is gules lined with argent, the colours of England and of the University.

In devising this group of arms Cooke figuratively took the University shield to pieces, and distributed its components among the Regius Professors. The ermine cross on red, and the red book (with the addition of the Greek letter theta) were assigned to the Professor of Divinity, the cross being placed between four doves. The Professors of Physic (or Medicine), Law, Hebrew and Greek each received one of the lions passant gardant, to be borne on a red

Physic or Medicine

Azure, a fesse ermines [*sic*, for ermine] betwene three Losenges gold, on a chiffe gules, a Lyon passant gardant gold, marked in his syde with this letter M sables; and for the Creast upon the healme, on a wreath gold and azure a Quinquangle Silver called *Simbolum sanitatis*; manteled gules doubled silver.

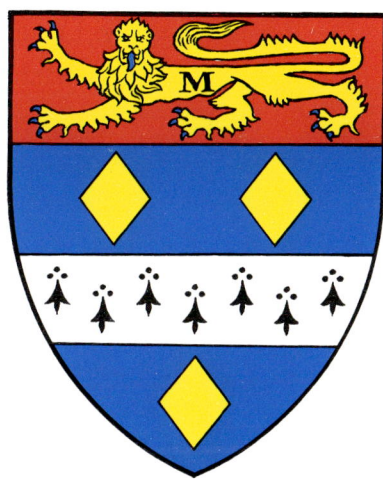

Law

The field purple, a Crosse molen gold, on a chiffe gules a Lyon passant gardant gold, marked in his syde with this letter L sables and to the Creast upon the healme, on a wreathe purple and gold a Bee volant gold; mantled gules doubled silver.

chief above other appropriate emblems, each lion being charged on its side with the initial letter of the subject of the professorship.

Cooke's patent illustrates the arms and crests in their heraldic tinctures. The document is in English. The blazons are given in their original spelling, but they have been punctuated for clarity.

Physic or Medicine

The lozenges represent medical remedies, the word having been used in this sense as early as 1530. The lion is appropriate to a King's Reader or Regius Professor of this University. It bears the letter M for Medicine. The quinquangle, a figure more commonly called a pentagram, was a symbol of health among the Pythagoreans, and was so regarded by Paracelsus (*c.*1490–1541).

At one time there was some doubt as to the tincture of the fess. In the patent it is described as 'ermines', which in early blazon is frequently found for 'ermine', i.e. black tufts on white, and the painting on the patent shows this fur. In later blazon the word 'ermines' has come to mean what was formerly termed 'erminees' i.e. white tufts on black. The record at the College of Arms, blazoning the fess as 'ermines', is not accompanied by a painting, and in 1967 the college held that the fess should be black with white tufts. However, in view of the painting in the patent, and other evidence that the fess has always been represented as ermine, the Kings of Arms eventually agreed that this fur might properly be used.

These arms, impaling those of Lorkin (*Ermine, three leopards' faces sable*), appear on a brass to the memory of Dr Lorkin in the Church of St Mary the Great.

Law

The cross is of the form termed 'moline' from its resemblance to the iron fastening at the centre of a millstone. The royal lion, from the arms of the University, is charged with the letter L for Law. That the bee was an accepted emblem of law and administration is shown by an extract from Gerard Legh's *Accedence of Armorie* (1562): 'Plinie saith, that a man may note a good government of a publique wealth, wisely maintained in perfit order under one prince by sundry officers, even in the little Bee.' Shakespeare used the same analogy in the passage in *Henry V* (I.ii) beginning:

> for so work the honey-bees,
> Creatures that by a rule in nature teach
> The act of order to a peopled kingdom.
> They have a king, and officers of sorts . . .

Divinity

The ermine cross on red, and the red book, are from the arms of the University, and the letter theta on the book stands for Theology. The doves in shield and crest have divine significance. Gerard Legh in his *Accedence of Armorie* stated: 'Isidore writeth, that the Dove is messenger of peace, which he brought between God and man, into the Arke of Noah, as plainly appeareth in Genesis. Christ likewise bad his Apostles (when he sent them out to preach) to be innocent as doves.'

Divinity

The field gules, on a Crosse ermen betwene foure
Doves silver, a Booke of the first, leaves gold,
clasped, noted in the midest with this Greke letter θ
Theta sables; and to the Creast upon the healme, on
a wreathe silver and gules a Dove volant silver with
an Olive braunche vert in his beke; manteled gules
doubled silver.

Hebrew

The field silver, the Hebrewe letter η Tawe sables, on a chiffe gules a Lyon passant gardant gold, marked in his syde with this letter H sables; and to the Creast upon the healme, on a wreathe silver and sables a Turtle Dove azure; manteled gules doubled silver.

Greek

The fielde silver and sables party per cheveron, in the first these two Greke letters *A* Alpha and *Ω* Omega sables, and in the seconde a Cicade or Gresshopper silver, on a chiffe gules a Lyon passant gardant gold marked on his side with this letter G sables; and to the Creast upon the healme, on a wreathe silver and sables an Owle silver, leges, beake and eares gold; manteled gules doubled silver.

Hebrew

Tāw, the last letter of the Hebrew alphabet, was probably included in the arms, not only as an indication of the subject of the Reader but also because of the significance it had for Christians. In the ancient Hebrew script this letter was written in the form of a cross, and for this reason the early Christians made much use of it (so the late Professor D. Winton Thomas in a private communication). Many of the Christian allusions to Tāw are based upon *Ezekiel* 9:4, where the heavenly writer puts a tāw, that is, a cross-shaped mark, upon the foreheads of those who were to be saved from the destroyers of Jerusalem. This passage in *Ezekiel* was connected by Christians, especially by St Jerome, with *Revelation* 7: 3–4. It was understood to refer to the sign of the cross with which Christians are either literally or metaphorically sealed, especially in baptism (so the late Professor G.W.H. Lampe in a private communication).

The royal lion from the arms of the University is marked with the letter H for Hebrew. The turtle dove presumably has its scriptural significance as an offering to God.

Greek

In addition to their obvious reference to Greek studies, the letters Alpha and Omega are an allusion to the Almighty as 'the first and the last' as in the *Book of Revelation*. The royal lion from the arms of the University bears the letter G for Greek. The 'Cicade or Gresshopper' – here apparently used as synonymous terms – is presumably the grasshopper worn as a symbol by the Athenians in token that they were born from the earth and had always lived in Attica. This is referred to by John Guillim in his *Display of Heraldrie* (1611):

'Among the Athenians the grashoppers were holden for a speciall note of Nobility; and therefore they used to weare golden Grashoppers in their haire (as Pierius noteth) to signifie thereby, that they were descended of noble race and homebred. For such is the naturall property of the Grashopper, that in what soile he is bred, in the same he will live and die, for they change not their place, nor hunt after new habitations'.

The owl is the emblem of Athens and Athena.

PETERHOUSE

Arms

D'or quatre pales ung bordre de gules semy
coronnes du champ [grant of 1575].
Or, four [or equally correctly, three] pales gules, a
bordure also gules charged with crowns or.

See of Ely

Second Peterhouse arms

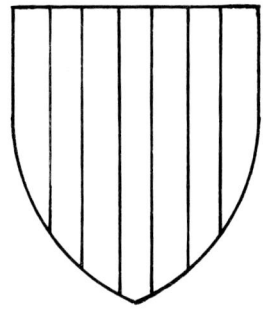

Hugh de Balsham

Peterhouse owes its origin to Hugh de Balsham, Bishop of Ely, and the shield combines the pales from his personal arms with crowns from the arms of the See of Ely. Previous bishops had exercised overall control of the students who settled in Cambridge during the first half of the thirteenth century, whose numbers increased as a result of events in Paris in 1229. In 1280, some years after the foundation of the Sorbonne in Paris and the experiment of Walter de Merton in Oxford, Hugh de Balsham by Royal Letters obtained licence to introduce into the Hospital of St John the Evangelist at Cambridge 'studious scholars who should in everything live together as students in the University of Cambridge according to the rule of the scholars at Oxford who are called of Merton'.

This hospital was an Augustinian institution founded in 1135 by Henry Frost, a worthy burgess of Cambridge. Here the scholars lived among the brethren, until Hugh removed them from the hospital to two hostels near the church of St Peter without Trumpington Gate (now St Mary the Less). This removal was confirmed by King Edward I at Westminster on 28 May 1284. It was also ordained that the scholars should be known as 'The Scholars of the Bishop of Ely'. The hostel came to be called the House of St Peter.

The college has used four different coats of arms, and the fourth (blazoned on page 30) appears in two versions.

The original seal (described later) includes a shield bearing three crowns, being the arms of the See of Ely: *Gules, three crowns or*. These were probably borne by leave of the founder, and marked the association of the college with the see. The arms are a differenced form of those attributed to the East Anglian royal house – *Azure, three crowns or* – and commemorate St Etheldreda, of that house, who founded the first monastery at Ely in 673.

The second coat is: *Gules, two keys in saltire or* – alluding to St Peter. These arms appear in Matthew Parker's *De Antiquitate Britannicae Ecclesiae* (in the compilation of which George Acworth, a fellow of the college, assisted) and his *Catalogus* (1572). An old panel portrait of the founder, reproduced by Ackerman in 1815, shows a shield on which the crowns of Ely are impaled with the crossed keys of St Peter.

A revised edition of Parker's *Catalogus* gives for the college: *Or, three pales gules* – the arms attributed to the founder. This is the third coat used by the college. It appears in Robert Hare's *Transcripts* (1587), and also in Hammond's map of 1592.

The fourth coat is the one blazoned at the head of this article. This was granted by Robert Cooke, Clarenceux King of Arms, in 1575. The arms were clearly based on those of the founder, but whereas he had borne three pales, Cooke, whether by oversight or as an intentional difference, granted the college four pales. The college promptly used the arms of Cooke's grant but with three pales, and continued to do so until 1866.

The version of the arms with three pales appeared in John Scott's book, 1617, and in various seventeenth-century maps and prints of Cambridge, and was allowed at the Visitation of 1684. An *Index of Arms*, at the time of Charles II, at the College of Arms gives the four pales coat of Cooke's grant with a marginal note: 'Mr. Gibbon Blew Mantle saies but three Pallets'. (Gibbon was a Cambridge man, of Jesus College.)

The original seal of the foundation was the earliest existing seal in the University when W.H. St John Hope took an impression from it in 1885. It has since been lost. It depicted the founder in bishop's vestments, holding his crosier in his left hand and with his right hand raised in benediction, between two tonsured scholars, one holding a book. Beneath the bishop's feet was a shield of the arms of the See of Ely, and above his head a trefoil arch supporting a half-length figure of St Peter holding two keys in the right hand and a book in the left. This seal was used until 1800, except during the Commonwealth period.

The puritan Lazarus Seaman, intruded as Master from 1644 to 1660, introduced a new seal, possibly on account of an objection to the former one on religious grounds, though it is also possible that John Cosin, the ousted Master, took the old seal with him while he was away from the college. The second seal bears a shield of the college arms showing three pales within a border charged with ten crowns, and above the shield the crossed keys of St Peter. This seal was readopted in 1800 and is still in use.

CLARE COLLEGE

Arms

Or, three chevrons gules [for CLARE], *impaling* Or, a cross gules [for DE BURGH]; all within a bordure sable goutty d'or.

The forerunner of the college was University Hall, established in 1326 by Richard de Badew, Chancellor of the University. On Hammond's map, 1592, 'Aula Universitatis' is represented by the arms attributed to Richard de Badew: *On a bend cotised three eagles displayed*. Within ten years the revenues of this hall, dependent on the University, proved to be insufficient, and greater endowments became necessary. These were provided by Elizabeth, Lady of Clare, by maternal descent a cousin of King Edward III, by whom she was encouraged in her benefaction. On 6 April 1338 Richard de Badew, as 'Founder, Patron and Advocate' of University Hall, formally placed it under its new patronage, but it seems to have retained its original name for at least two more years. De Badew made a second complete surrender of all his interests in his foundation in 1346, and thereafter it was known as Clare Hall, and as Clare College after 1856.

Lady Elizabeth (*c*.1292–1360) was one of the three daughters of Gilbert de Clare IV, Earl of Gloucester and Hertford, and Joan of Acre, daughter of King Edward I and Eleanor of Castile. The male line of the House of Clare, which had great power and influence from the time of the Norman Conquest, came to an end in 1314 when Gilbert V (son of Gilbert IV) was slain at Bannockburn leaving no surviving children. His sisters became co-heiresses to the great Clare inheritance, and to Elizabeth fell the title 'Lady of Clare'. She married three times and was thrice widowed. Her first husband was John de Burgh, heir to the earldom of Ulster. Dying in 1313, he did not live to inherit, but his son William succeeded as Earl in due course. The Lady Elizabeth's second husband, Theobald Lord Verdun, died in 1316, and her third husband, Roger Lord Damory, died in 1322.

The arms borne by Clare College are derived from the foundress's first marriage. When the arms of man and wife are impaled, the husband's coat is normally placed on the dexter side of the shield. However, in the foundress's arms the Clare coat holds the dexter position, the Lady of Clare having had in her own right an honour and inheritance superior to that of John de Burgh. The coats are encircled by a black border sprinkled with golden tears, which the Lady Elizabeth adopted as a sign of mourning after the death of her third husband.

These were confirmed as the 'ancient arms' of the college at the Visitations of 1575 and 1684. They fittingly commemorate not only the foundress herself but also the House of Clare. This continued after the failure of the male line, for the Lady Elizabeth's son, William Earl of Ulster, had a daughter Elizabeth who married Lionel of Antwerp, Edward III's third son, and brought him the Clare domains, or 'Clarence', and in 1362 he was created Duke of Clarence. In *Heralds of England* (1967) Sir Anthony Wagner, sometime Garter and now Clarenceux King of Arms, observed that the latter heraldic title was derived from heraldic service to the House of Clare.

The common seal of the college shows the foundress presenting her charter of refoundation to the representatives of the college kneeling around her. On either side there is a shield, the dexter of England and the sinister of Castile and Leon quarterly – the arms of her royal grandparents; while another shield in the base bears the arms of Clare impaling de Burgh within a border goutty, showing that the arms now borne by the college were personal to the foundress in her lifetime.

The recent practice of placing an earl's coronet above the arms of the college or using a modern earl's coronet as the badge is quite incorrect.

There is an heraldic link between Clare College and Merton College, Oxford, which bears the personal arms of its founder, Walter de Merton, Bishop of Rochester, namely: *Or, three chevrons, the first and third per pale azure and gules and the second per pale gules and azure.* These arms, based on the shield of the Clare family, were assumed by Walter de Merton because two of the de Clare Earls of Gloucester assisted him in the foundation of the college.

PEMBROKE COLLEGE

Arms

Barry of ten argent and azure, an orle of martlets gules [for DE VALENCE] *dimidiating* Gules, three pales vair, on a chief or, a label of five points azure [for DE ST POL].

These, the arms of the foundress, form part of the design on the original seal of the college. They are given as the arms of the college in Archbishop Parker's *Catalogus* (1572), and at the Heralds' Visitation of 1684 they were recorded as the 'ancient arms' of the college, borne of right.

The college was founded in 1347 by Mary de St Pol, Countess of Pembroke. She was the daughter of Guy, Count of St Pol in the Pas de Calais, and great-great-granddaughter of Isabel of Angoulême by her first marriage to John, King of England. In 1321 Mary became the second wife of Aymer de Valence, Earl of Pembroke, who was himself a great-grandson of Isabel of Angoulême by her second marriage to Hugh le Brun, Lord of Lusignan. In the foundress's arms, the coats of de Valence and de St Pol were combined by dimidiation; that is, the two shields are figuratively cut down the middle, and the dexter half of the husband's shield is joined to the sinister half of the wife's. (In practice, slightly more than half of a coat may be shown in dimidiation, and the illustration accordingly shows two complete pales and three points of the label in the de St Pol half.)

Aymer de Valence died in 1324. In her widowhood the Countess of Pembroke, from the resources of her large estates, founded and made benefactions to several abbeys. In September 1342 she bought from Hervey de Stanton a strip of land running south from Trumpington Street along the outside of the King's Ditch on which to found a college. A royal licence for the foundation of what was first called the 'House of Valence-Marie' was signed by Edward III on Christmas Eve 1347, and the charter from the foundress is dated 9 June 1348.

The original seal (*c.*1347) shows the figures of Aymer de Valence and the foundress, each holding up a hand towards a conventional representation of the college, and standing between two shields, each hanging from a tree. The dexter shield bears the arms of de Valence, and the sinister one de Valence dimidiating de St Pol.

Burelly argent and azure, the coat of the house of Lusignan, was differenced by Valence with *an orle of martlets gules* as borne by Aymer's father, William de Valence, in the latter part of his life. While the college arms normally show *barry of ten*, the coat is found with more or fewer bars and a variable number of martlets. The shield borne by the effigy of William de Valence in Westminster Abbey has 28 bars and 19 martlets. The de St Pol arms are those of the great house of Chatillon, differenced with *a label azure* by Guy de St Pol as the head of a younger branch. They form a quartering in the shield of Queen Elizabeth Woodville (see Queens' College).

Mary de St Pol,
after a seal in the British Museum

GONVILLE AND CAIUS COLLEGE

Arms

Argent, on a chevron between two couple closes indented sable three escallops or [for GONVILLE] *impaling*, Or semy of flowers gentle, in the middle of the chief a sengrene resting upon the heads of two serpents in pale, their tails knit together, all in proper colour, resting upon a square marble stone vert, between their breasts a book sable garnished gules, buckles or [for CAIUS]; all within a bordure compony argent and sable.

Edmund Gonville

The name and armorial bearings of Gonville and Caius College commemorate equally the two men chiefly concerned in its foundation – Edmund Gonville, Rector of Terrington near Lynn, the first founder, and Dr John Caius, the third founder. Bishop Bateman, who ranks as second founder because he completed and amplified Gonville's intentions, has heraldic commemoration in his own separate foundation of Trinity Hall.

The college was first founded in 1348 as Gonville Hall. A site was acquired on the narrow strip of land now occupied by the Master's garden at Corpus Christi, and a body of statutes was drawn up. However, Gonville died in 1351, and Bishop Bateman, his friend and executor, drew up a new set of statutes, changed the name to the Hall of the Annunciation of the Blessed Virgin Mary, and removed the college to its present site next to Trinity Hall. The only known seal of the first foundation represents the Annunciation of the Virgin within a canopy, with Bishop Bateman and others.

It is not known whether the Hall used arms. If so, they would presumably have been those of Edmund Gonville. These appear to have differed from the coat attributed to Gonville and incorporated in the arms (blazoned on page 42) granted to the college in 1575. Dr John Venn, sometime President of Caius, discussed this in *The Caian* (vol. xviii, 1909, pp. 121–134). Mill Stephenson and Z.N.B[rooke] took this up in another article in *The Caian* (vol. xli, 1933, pp. 59–65).

John Caius (originally spelt Kees), a native of Norwich, graduated from Gonville Hall in 1533, and later studied medicine at Padua and graduated M.D. Returning to London, he was elected President of the College of Physicians. On offering indirectly to endow Gonville Hall, he discovered that it had never been properly incorporated, and he duly obtained a Royal Charter of foundation and confirmation of past acts on 4 September 1557. This renamed the hall Gonville and Caius College. Soon afterwards Dr Caius was elected Master, and retained this position until shortly before his death.

In January 1560–61 Caius obtained from Laurence Dalton, Norroy King of Arms, a grant of the complicated coat which now forms the sinister half of the college shield, together with the crest of *a dove argent beaked and membered gules holding in his beak by the stalk a flower gentle in proper colour, stalked vert*. The grant goes on to explain the meaning of the coat, and it has been assumed that the explanation was furnished by Dr Caius himself:

'betokening by the boke learning, by the ii serpentes resting upon the square marble stone, wisdome with grace founded and stayed upon vertues stable stone; by sengrene and flower gentile, immortality y^t never shall fade, as though thus I shulde saye, ex prudentia et literis, virtutis, petra firmatis immortalitas, that is to say by wisdome and lerning graffed in grace and vertue, men cum to immortalite.'

While the sengrene (the houseleek in flower) and flowers gentle (floramor) were expressly introduced as emblems of immortality, their remedial significance must also have commended them to Dr Caius.

Parker's *Catalogus* gives as the arms of the college Gonville impaling Caius without a border. From the heraldic point of view the joining of two coats by simple impalement would suggest a marriage between members of the two families. Accordingly at the Visitation of 1575 Robert Cooke, Clarenceux King of Arms, thought it proper to correct such an impression, and to combine the coats of the founders in such a way as to create a unified and distinctive shield for the foundation. This he did by surrounding the impaled arms by a border of the tinctures of the Gonville coat. His grant, after a brief preamble, continues:

'In consideration whereof and for a perpetuall memory of their founders, Edmund Gonvile and John Caius, I have sett foorth and graunted to Thomas Legg, doctor of the civile law and maister of the saide colledg, the fellowes and scollers of the same and their successors for ever this shilde of Armes hereafter following That is to saye the Armes of the aforesaide Gonvile and Caius in pale [i.e. impaled] within a Border gobone silver and sables.'

TRINITY HALL

Arms
Sable, a crescent within a bordure ermine.

Crest
On a wreath argent and sable, a lion sejant gules holding a book, the cover sable, the leaves or; mantling, gules doubled argent.

Trinity Hall was founded in 1350 by William Bateman, Bishop of Norwich, on the site of a hostel of the monks of Ely. The foundation was designed especially for the study of canon and civil law, in which Bateman had made his mark, and the traditional connection between Trinity Hall and law still continues. The college received a Royal Charter from King Edward III in 1351.

The founder's arms, which appear on his seal, were: *[Sable], a crescent ermine within a bordure engrailed [argent]*. According to an entry in the Master's Statute Book (since lost, but thought by Warren, who transcribed it, to be in the hand of Henry Hervey, the Master at whose instance the present arms were granted in 1575) Bateman's father had borne three crescents; these arms passed to his eldest son, while the second son bore two crescents, and the third son one crescent, for difference. However, evidence so long after the event should be treated with caution.

For a considerable time the arms of the founder were used by the college, and they appear on the old seals. On the original great seal of the college, and also on the Master's seal, these arms are placed beneath a representation of the Holy Trinity. There is also a small seal bearing Bateman's arms with a contracted inscription showing it to have been that of Stephen Gardiner, Master from 1525 to 1549 and again from 1553 to 1555. The founder's coat thus appears to have been used by the college from the foundation until the granting of the present arms.

In the founder's statutes of 1352 there is a provision that books shall be marked with a device, illustrated in the statutes, which may be blazoned: *Sable, between the points of a crescent ermine a cross paty argent.*

About 1559 Henry Hervey became Master of Trinity Hall, and at his instigation Robert Cooke, Clarenceux King of Arms, in 1575 granted the armorial bearings blazoned at the head of this article. The arms granted to the college were differenced from those of the founder by changing his silver engrailed border to a plain border of ermine. The grant of a crest to an academic body at this date was not common, though other instances are found in the grants to Queens' College and Jesus College.

The representation of the college arms on the west wall of the library corresponds closely with the illustration in the margin of the patent. It was described by Warren as 'Founder's arms: in clunch, almost worn out', but has since been restored and repainted.

A common error in the past has been to confuse the college arms with those of the founder and to show them: *Sable, a crescent*  *within a bordure engrailed ermine.* For example, they appear thus on a bookplate made by one Jackson in 1700.

CORPUS CHRISTI COLLEGE

Arms

Quarterly: 1 and 4, Gules, a pelican in its piety argent; 2 and 3, Azure, three lily flowers argent.

The college is the outcome of the union of two guilds of Cambridge townsfolk, one of Corpus Christi and the other of the Blessed Virgin Mary. These combined in 1350, and in 1352 the united guild founded a college called 'Domus Scholarium Corporis Christi et Beatae Mariae Virginis'. It also had what Thomas Fuller called a 'working day name' *viz*. Benet College, from its proximity to St Benet's Church, where the members worshipped before the college chapel was built.

Until the Reformation the college used the shields of the two guilds: that of the Blessed Virgin Mary being the floral emblem of the Holy Trinity, and that of Corpus Christi displaying the Crown of Thorns and other instruments of the Passion. These, with a depiction of the coronation of the Virgin, and a representation of the college, appear on the common seal, which probably dates from the foundation.

Robert Masters, in *The History of the College of Corpus Christi and the Blessed Virgin Mary, commonly called Bene't, in the University of Cambridge, from its foundation to the present time* (1753), wrote: 'At the beginning of the Reformation, some people had taken offence at the arms of the college . . . thinking them superstitious by reason of our Saviour's standing over the two shields . . . and crowning the Virgin Mary.' To remedy this, Matthew Parker 'was at the expense of obtaining new ones from the Heralds' Office . . . these still seem to have some allusion to the ancient Gilds united in this foundation'. The pelican 'in its piety', i.e. feeding its young with blood drawn from its own breast, represents Christ shedding his blood for His elect, and is a symbol of Corpus Christi, while the three lilies denote the virginity of Mary. The charges combined in the new arms were more appropriate to the names of the two guilds than the symbols on their earlier shields.

Archbishop Parker procured the grant of the new arms in 1570 from Robert Cooke, Clarenceux King of Arms. Parker had been Master of Corpus Christi between 1544 and 1553, and earlier he had been dean of the college of priests attached to the church of Stoke by Clare in Suffolk, the dissolution of which in 1548 he tried in vain to prevent. Masters states that Parker regarded the lilies in the college arms not only as signifying the Guild of the Blessed Virgin, but also as having the secondary significance 'of preserving the memory of his favourite college of Stoke'. Their relevance to Stoke lay in the fact that associated with that college there was a chapel of the Blessed Virgin of Stoke, providing a stipend for one of the prebendaries, and the mass of Our Lady was to be sung daily by the college.

The patent of arms issued by Clarenceux Cooke is in Latin, and describes the arms: *'per singulas quartas scuti partes approbare in prima videlicet gules Pellicanum cum suis pullis argentes nido cubantibus in secunda quarta asuer tria lilia argentea, eademque ratione per singulas quartas'*.

The college possesses a fine carving of a pelican in its piety which has recently been restored and re-silvered, and has been placed in the hall.

KING'S COLLEGE

Arms

Sable, three roses argent, a chief per pale azure and gules charged on the dexter side with a fleur-de-lis and on the sinister with a lion passant gardant or.

The roses, blazoned argent in the grant, are frequently represented as barbed vert and seeded or.

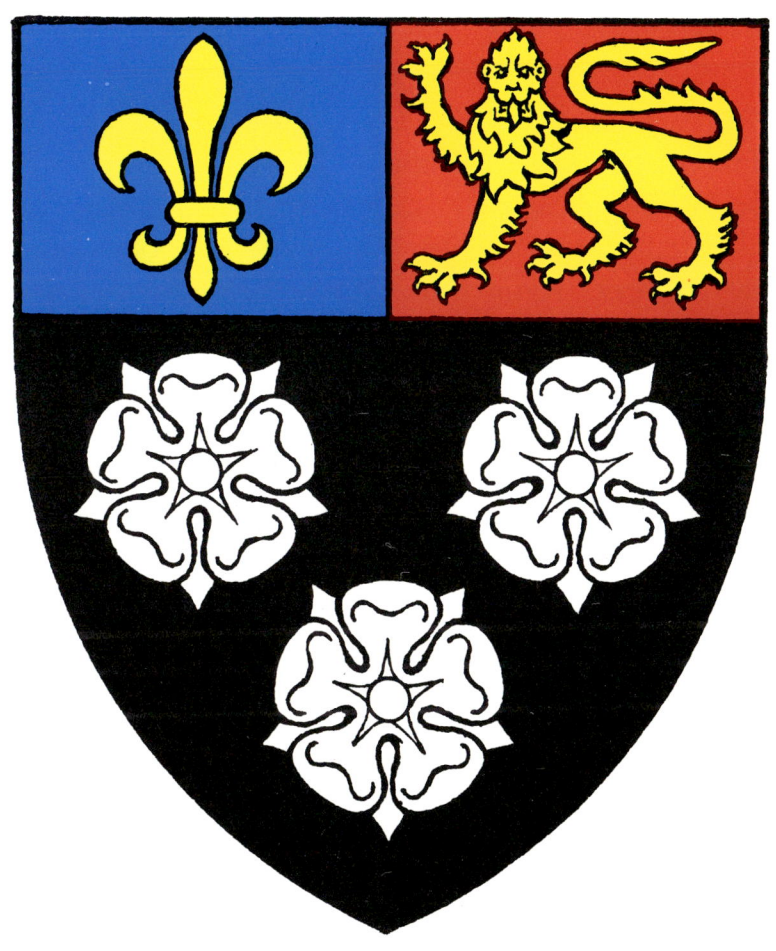

The college was founded by King Henry VI. On Passion Sunday 1441 he personally laid the first stone of a building for a college to be dedicated to St Nicholas, but the original site proved to be insufficient so in 1443 it was enlarged and the college was reconstituted as 'the King's College of St Mary and St Nicholas', linked with Henry's other collegiate foundation, St Mary of Eton.

Arms were granted to the college by letters patent dated 1 January 1448/9. The document, on which the arms are depicted in the centre, is in Latin. The passage describing and explaining the arms was translated as follows by Henry Bradshaw, Fellow of King's and University Librarian, for W.H. St John Hope and published in the proceedings of the Cambridge Antiquarian Society, 1894:

'Therefore we assign for arms and ensigns of arms, in a field sable three silver roses, having in mind that our newly founded College, to last for ages to come, whose perpetuity we wish to be signified by the stability of the black colour, may bring forth the brightest flowers redolent of every kind of knowledge to the honour and most devout worship of Almighty God, and the spotless Virgin and glorious Mother, to whom as in other things so especially in this our foundation, with an ardent mind we offer our heartfelt and most earnest devotion. To which also that we may impart something of royal nobility which may declare the work truly royal and illustrious, portions of the arms which by royal right belong to us in the Kingdoms of England and France, we have appointed to be placed in the chief of the shield party per pale of azure with a flower of the French and of gules with a leopard passant gold.'

On the same day letters patent were issued to Eton College, granting similar arms but for the substitution of 'three lily flowers silver' for the roses.

Before 1448 King's College bore arms consisting of two lily flowers (for St Mary) and in base a pastoral staff encircled by a mitre (for St Nicholas) with a chief charged with a fleur-de-lis and a lion as in the later arms. This coat may be seen on impressions of the first college seal and in glass in the chapel.

Eton
College

King's before
1448

QUEENS' COLLEGE

Arms

Quarterly of six: 1, Barry of eight argent and gules [for HUNGARY]; 2, Azure semy of fleurs-de-lis or, a label of three points gules [for ANJOU ANCIENT or NAPLES]; 3, Argent, a cross potent between four crosses crosslet potent or [for JERUSALEM]; 4, Azure semy of fleurs-de-lis or, a bordure gules [for ANJOU MODERN]; 5, Azure semy of crosses crosslet fitchy, two barbels haurient addorsed or [for BAR]; 6, Or, on a bend gules three alerions displayed argent [for LORRAINE]; all within a bordure vert.

Crest

Out of a coronet or, an eagle rousant sable, wings or; mantled gules doubled argent.

The arms are those of Margaret of Anjou, Queen to Henry VI, differenced by a border. They were granted to the college in this form in 1575.

In 1446 Andrew Dokett, Rector of St Botolph's and Principal of St Bernard's Hostel, obtained from the King a charter of incorporation for the College of St Bernard, but the site first chosen proved unsuitable and a new charter was signed in 1447 refounding the college on its present site. Soon afterwards Queen Margaret petitioned her husband that she might take over the responsibility for the foundation and, the King approving, on 15 April 1448 she issued her charter of foundation to 'The Queen's College of St Margaret and St Bernard'.

Seventeen years later Elizabeth Woodville, a former lady-in-waiting to Queen Margaret, and now by her second marriage Queen to Edward IV, succeeded to the patronage of the college, and she granted its first statutes in 1475. Anne Neville, Queen to Richard III – himself a benefactor of the college – also acted as patroness. However, not until the nineteenth century was the apostrophe in the name moved to make it Queens' College.

Andrew Dokett came of a Westmorland family which bore: *Sable, a saltire argent*. These arms commemorate him in various parts of the college, but he did not place them on his seal and the college does not appear to have used them in its corporate insignia.

The first seal, given by Henry VI to the College of St Bernard in 1446, bore the Royal Arms. The second, granted in 1448 by Queen Margaret, bore the arms which she derived from her father René, Duke of Anjou, of Lorraine and of Bar, and titular King of Naples, Sicily and Jerusalem. The six quarterings represent these lordships and dignities, and also René's descent from the first house of Anjou and thereby a claim to the crown of Hungary. The quartering for Jerusalem (representing a non-existent kingdom but a title of high prestige) is of heraldic interest because the crosses are gold on a silver field. This unusual combination reflects the colours of the Papal banner held by Eustace of Boulogne in the Bayeux tapestry. His descendants were among the first rulers of the Crusaders' kingdom of Jerusalem, and René of Anjou was among the claimants to it.

Andrew Dokett

Queen Elizabeth
Woodville's arms

Alternative arms to
those of Queen Margaret

The third seal used by the college was given in 1465 by Elizabeth Woodville. It bore her arms together with those of Edward IV, and in base a shield charged with a cross and in the first quarter a sword erect. Even without the colours, this is identifiable as the arms of the City of London. As there was no connection between the college and the city, this shield has long presented a problem. However, Mr J. Bromley, sometime Librarian of the Guildhall Library, has pointed out that both Elizabeth Woodville and Margaret of Anjou were 'sisters' of the Skinners' Company, which used the city shield before it obtained arms of its own, and the shield presumably represents the royal patroness in this capacity. It does not follow, as Atkinson and Clark have suggested in their *Cambridge Described and Illustrated* (1897), p. 375, that the college was once entitled to make use of the arms of the City of London.

A fourth seal, of which no trace or impression survives, is referred to in an inventory of the college plate in 1544: '*Item antiquum sigillum argenteum ex dono Ricardi Sčdi R. Anglie insculptum porcellis seu apris.*' ('*Secundi*', abbreviated to '*sčdi*', is obviously a mistake for '*tertii*'.) This entry is the earliest evidence of a long tradition at Queens' of the use of a white boar's head (derived from Richard III's badge of a silver boar) surmounting a cross for St Margaret and a crozier for St Bernard, both gold and placed saltirewise. Today this device is used by many college clubs. Formerly, placed on a sable shield, it was used as an alternative coat of arms to that of Queen Margaret, at least as early as Matthew Parker's *Catalogus* of 1572, and even after the grant of arms in 1575. However, it has never appeared on a college seal.

There is no conclusive evidence as to which coat was more often used at the time of the Visitation by Robert Cooke, Clarenceux King of Arms, in 1575, but he evidently regarded the arms of Queen Margaret as appropriate to the college. The patent which he issued declared that the Queen not only incorporated the college but 'did also graunt unto the saide President and fellowes and their successors her armes to be used in the saide colledge as they stande depicted in this margent'. He went on to blazon the arms of Queen Margaret with the important addition of a 'a border vert', evidently intended as a difference, though he did not mention this. He then granted the crest 'for divers good considerations me moving, and at the request of William Chadderton now doctor of divinitie and President of the saide colledge'.

In some details Cooke's blazon of Queen Margaret's arms is not in accordance with the second seal of the college and other contemporary evidence. In the second quartering he blazons the label argent instead of gules; in the third he omits to describe the four crosslets as potent, though they are so shown in the marginal painting; in the fifth he fails to state that the crosses crosslet are fitchy, and describes the barbels (allusive to Bar) as luces; and in the sixth he uses the word eagles for the birds which in the arms of Lorraine are usually termed alerions. In the arms used by the college these discrepancies have been amended, and a corrected blazon appears at the head of this article.

The arms of Queen Elizabeth Woodville were: *Quarterly of six: 1, Argent, a lion rampant double-queued gules crowned or* (for LUXEMBURG); *2, Quarterly, i and iv, Gules, an estoile argent; ii and iii, France Ancient* (for BAUX); *3, Barry of ten argent and azure, a lion rampant gules* (for CYPRUS); *4, Gules, three bends argent, on a chief per fess argent and or a rose gules* (for URSINS); *5, Gules, three pales vair, on a chief or a label of five points azure* (for ST POL); *6, Argent, a fess and a canton conjoined gules* (for WOODVILLE). The first five quarterings were derived from her mother, Jacquetta of Luxemburg, daughter of Peter, Count of St Pol. The arms of St Pol are also found in the shield of Pembroke College.

St Catharine's College

Arms

Gules, a Catherine wheel or [for ST CATHARINE].

The college, originally called St Catharine's Hall, was founded in 1473 by Robert Woodlarke, Provost of King's College.

The wheel set with knives or spikes is the emblem of St Catharine of Alexandria who, according to the Revd E.E. Dorling's *Heraldry of the Church* (1911) 'was universally reverenced as the patroness of learning and as the noblest type of chastity . . . Her persecutors strove to put her to death by breaking her upon a wheel set with spikes, which by divine interposition was broken.' In Christian art the wheel of St Catharine is commonly represented as broken, but in the shield assigned to her, as in the arms of the college, it is shown whole.

The earliest known representations of the college arms are in a late sixteenth-century manuscript in the College of Arms and in Matthew Parker's *Catalogus* (1572). At the Visitation of Cambridge by Sir Henry St George, Clarenceux King of Arms, in 1684 the arms were recorded as 'ancientlie borne and used' by the college, and in the St Catharine's accounts for 1683–4 there is an entry: 'Laid out by ye Master to Sir Fr. St George for registering ye college armes & seal . . . £1.10.0.'

The number of spokes and knives in the Catherine wheel is not specified in the blazon of the arms, and in various representations six, eight or even twelve spokes appear, and any number of knives. However, the record at the College of Arms of the 1684 Heralds' Visitation shows eight spokes with eight knives in line with them, and in 1934 A.J. Toppin, then York Herald, advised the use of this form.

Seal in use from 1475

The college seal represents St Catharine kneeling with a sword on one side and a wheel on the other.

The personal arms of Robert Woodlarke were: *Per bend indented azure and gules, in sinister chief a fleur-de-lis and in dexter base a lion passant gardant or* – a coat evidently derived from the charges on the chief of the King's College shield. Bishop G. Forrest Browne, in his history of the college (1902), maintained that the college originally bore these arms impaled with the Catherine wheel coat. A.C. Fox-Davies in *The Book of Public Arms* (1915) attributed to the college the arms of Woodlarke with the Catherine wheel as a crest, quoting as his authority the University Calendar. While these represent former variations in the heraldic practice of the college, it is now commonly agreed that there was no authority for them.

Robert Woodlarke

JESUS COLLEGE

Arms
Argent, a fess between three cocks' heads erased
sable, combed and wattled gules, within a bordure
gules semy of crowns or.

Crest
Out of a coronet or, a cock sable membered gules;
mantled gules doubled silver.

Motto
PROSPERUM ITER FACIAS

The college was founded in 1496 by John Alcock, Bishop of Ely, as the College of the Blessed Virgin Mary, St John the Evangelist and the Glorious Virgin St Radegund on the site of the old priory of St Radegund, which had 'become delapidated and wasted' owing to the improvidence of the nuns (letters patent quoted in Stubbs's *Cambridge*). It was commonly known from its foundation as Jesus College. The original shield used by the college was probably the 'Five Wounds' (the pierced heart, hands and feet of Christ), shown held by an angel in the base of the common seal. This was abandoned at the Reformation, probably as 'giving offence' (like the first arms of Corpus Christi College), but it may be seen in a modern representation over the archway from Chapel Court to Pump Court.

Matthew Parker's *Catalogus* (1572) shows for Jesus College the present arms with the addition of a gold mitre on the fess, and college plate shows that the arms in this form were in general use in the sixteenth century.

In 1575, Robert Cooke, Clarenceux King of Arms, granted the college a crest as an addition to the arms 'of longe tyme borne', and in the process he redefined the arms, omitting the mitre from the fess. In the patent the arms are blazoned: '*silver a fesse bettwen thre cocks heads razed sables combid and watled a border gules semy crowns golde*', and the crest '*upon the helme out of a crowne golde a cocke sables membred gules, mantled gules doubled silver*'. The arms are shown thus on the 'Ad Causas' seal of 1586, but the shield is still commonly seen with the mitre on the fess, as for example in the ceiling of the Jesus gate tower.

Basically the arms are those of John Alcock and are allusive to his name. As his father was a burgess of Hull they are not likely to have any earlier history. The mitre on the fess was personal to John Alcock, marking his position as a bishop; his nephew, Master of Jesus in 1515–16, bore the arms without a mitre. The red border with gold crowns is from the arms of the See of Ely: *Gules, three crowns or* – commemorating St Etheldreda, a lady of the East Anglian royal house, to which three gold crowns on blue were assigned as arms. Cooke granted a similar border to Peterhouse.

The illustration in the margin of Cooke's patent shows ten crowns on the border, but in modern usage it is more common to show only eight. The motto, PROSPERUM ITER FACIAS (literally, 'may you make a prosperous journey' – *bon voyage!*), while not mentioned in the grant, sometimes appears on a scroll below the arms, as on the Memorial Gates on Victoria Avenue. The arms are displayed on both sides of the gateway at the Jesus Lane end of the 'Chimney', and on each side the three cocks' heads are shown looking westward, with the result that the heads on the college side of the gate face to the sinister, which is heraldically unusual.

We, the editors, give way to temptation here to record that the late Frederick (Freddy) Brittain (1893–1969), for many years a fellow of Jesus, left among the treasures of his college a most remarkable collection of cocks of all sizes and materials. He was for a long time senior treasurer of the University Heraldic Society and saw the beginnings of this present work.

The 'Five Wounds'

CHRIST'S COLLEGE AND ST JOHN'S COLLEGE

Arms

Quarterly; 1 and 4, Azure, three fleurs-de-lis or [for
FRANCE MODERN]; 2 and 3, Gules, three lions
passant gardant in pale or [for ENGLAND]; all
within a bordure compony argent and azure.

These colleges both have the same arms, those of their foundress, the Lady
Margaret Beaufort. They are given in Matthew Parker's *Catalogus* (1572) as
the arms of the two colleges, but were not recorded as such at either the
Visitation of 1575 or that of 1684. In displays of the foundress's heraldry in the
colleges, the following are also found:

Crest

Out of a coronet, a demi eagle displayed gorged
with a crown or.

Supporters

Two yales argent bezanty, armed, unguled and
tufted or.

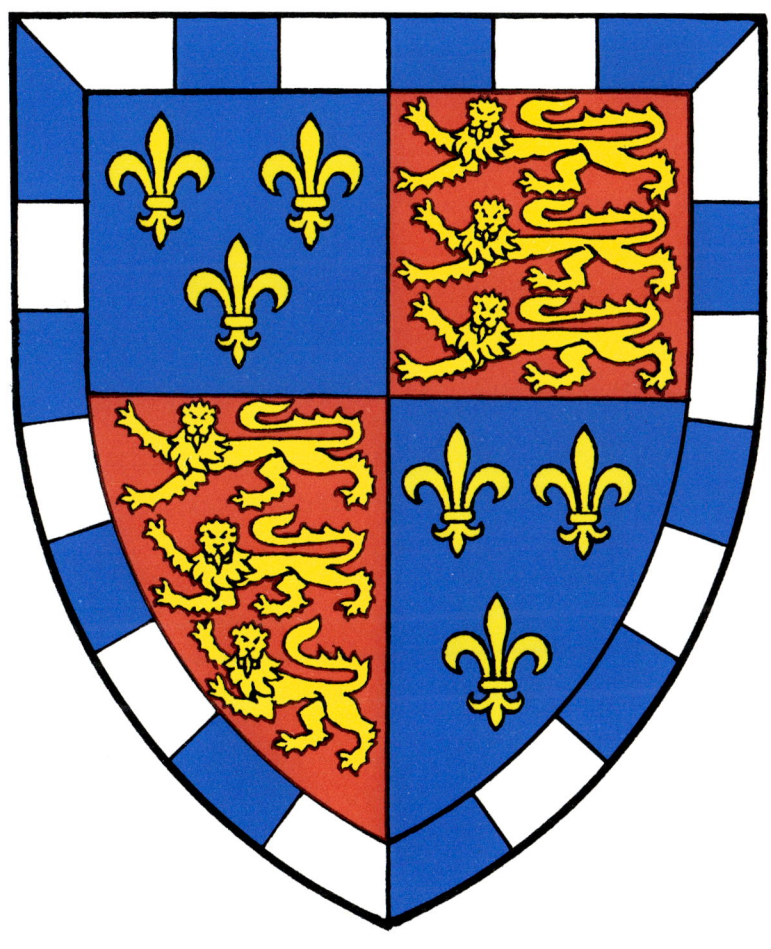

The Lady Margaret Beaufort, Countess of Richmond and Derby (1443–1509), founded Christ's College in 1505, and put in hand the foundation of the College of St John the Evangelist which was completed in 1511 by her executor, John Fisher, Bishop of Rochester. She also established the Lady Margaret Professorship of Divinity. The Beaufort family derived from the union of John of Gaunt, Duke of Lancaster, and Catherine Swynford, who later became his third wife, whereupon their children were legitimated. The eldest son of this union was John Beaufort who was created Earl of Somerset. Lady Margaret was his granddaughter, and her son came to the throne as Henry VII.

The arms of the Beauforts, after their legitimation, were the Royal Arms of England in the form they took from 1401, with a border for difference. The *three lions passant gardant* had become the arms of England in the reign of Richard I. In 1340, Edward III, in token of his claim to the French throne, quartered in his shield the Royal Arms of France, then *Azure semy of fleurs-de-lis or* (called France Ancient). Later King Charles V of France reduced the number of fleurs-de-lis to three (France Modern), and in 1403 Henry IV of England made this change in his Royal Arms.

The Beauforts bore these quartered arms, differenced by a border of the Lancastrian colours silver and blue, blazoned as *compony argent and azure*. This means that along the top of the shield the first division on the dexter side is argent, the second azure, and so on. In the arms of some members of the Beaufort family the border is found starting with a blue division (i.e. *compony azure and argent*), but in representations of Lady Margaret's arms, and on her father's stall-plate in St George's Chapel, Windsor, as a Knight of the Garter, *compony argent and azure*. This is the form used by the two colleges.

Variations are found in the number of pieces into which the border is divided. Attempts have been made to distinguish between the arms of the colleges by giving Christ's a border *compony* of more and smaller pieces than St John's, but there is no authority for this.

Lady Margaret's father used as a supporter a gold crowned eagle derived from a badge of Edward III, and a silver yale with gold spots. The yale is a deer-like creature supposed to be able to swivel its horns, which are therefore often represented as curving in opposite directions. It was perhaps a variant of the heraldic antelope which was a Lancastrian badge. In Lady Margaret's heraldry, the gold eagle was used as a crest and two yales as supporters.

In achievements of the foundress's heraldry over the gateway and on an oriel outside the master's lodge of each college, the arms were accompanied by badges – the portcullis of Beaufort and the red rose of Lancaster. Above the portcullis there is a coronet, while the rose is ensigned by a royal crown – not applicable to Lady Margaret herself, but a token that in her son a descendant of John of Gaunt, and thus of Edward III, had come to the throne. (Henry VII on his marriage with Elizabeth of York combined the roses of Lancaster and York to form the Tudor rose of red and white.) In the background of these achievements, marguerites, allusive to the foundress's Christian name, are liberally used, and on St John's gate tower the coronet above the shield is composed of these flowers. On the oriel at Christ's the arms are accompanied by the words: SOUVENT ME SOUVIENT (Call me often to mind).

It is remarkable that the arms of these colleges were not placed on record at Robert Cooke's Visitation of 1575, since Cooke was a member of St John's and would surely have had a special interest in the heraldry of his own college. However, as has been shown in the Introduction, as a general rule Cooke made some addition to the arms of a founder to create a distinctive coat for the foundation. He would have had good reason to do this in the case of these two colleges, since the Beaufort arms were still extant, being borne by the Somerset Earls of Worcester, though they marked their illegitimate descent from the Beaufort Dukes of Somerset by bearing the Beaufort coat on a fess. It may be that Cooke proposed to grant a differenced form of the Beaufort arms to Christ's and St John's, but that the colleges, with their foundress's heraldry prominently displayed on their buildings, rejected any alteration. Whatever the reason, the Beaufort arms were never confirmed for use by the two colleges. At the present time the Duke of Beaufort, descended from the Earls of Worcester, bears the undifferenced arms of Beaufort.

MAGDALENE COLLEGE

Arms

Quarterly per pale indented or and azure, in the
second and third quarters an eagle displayed or,
over all on a bend azure a fret between two
martlets or.

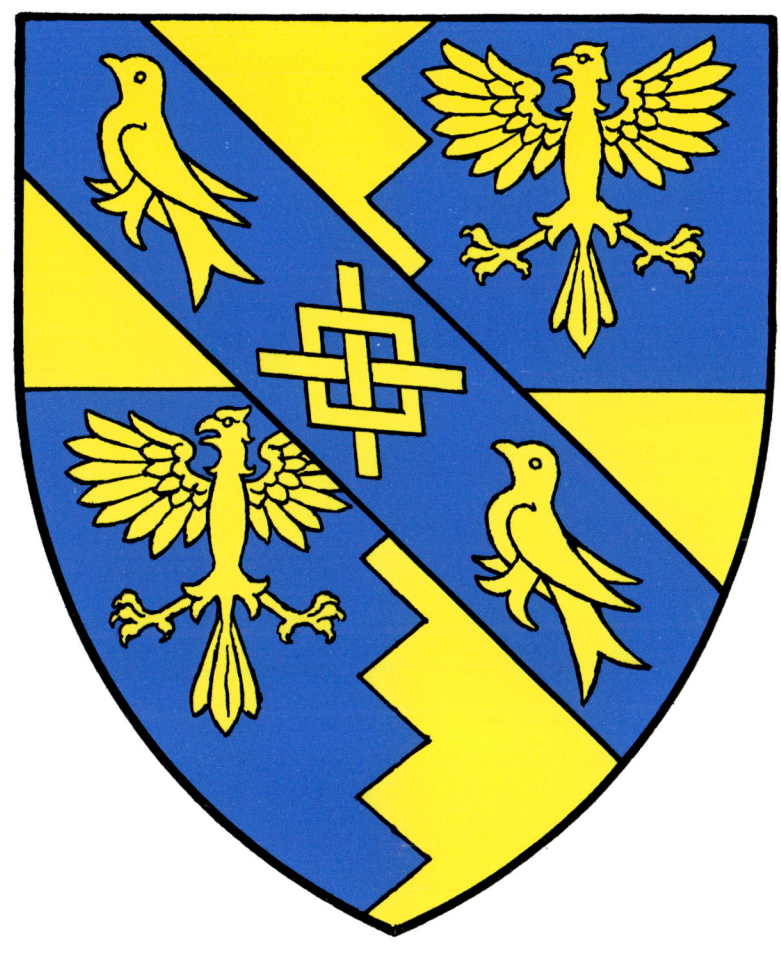

These are the arms of the founder, Thomas, Lord Audley of Walden. They are given as the arms of the college in Parker's *Catalogus* (1572), Hare's *Transcripts* (1587), Hammond's map (1592) and in later records, but their use has not been formally allowed by the Kings of Arms.

The forerunner of the college was a Benedictine hostel established in 1428 by Croyland Abbey, and from 1483 (and perhaps earlier) this hostel was known as Buckingham College, presumably on account of a benefaction by a Duke of Buckingham, although the details of this are unknown.

In April 1542 Buckingham College was refounded as 'The College of St Mary Magdalene' by Thomas, Lord Audley of Walden, Lord Chancellor and a former Speaker of the House of Commons, a member of an Essex family. The arms blazoned above were granted to Audley when he became a baron in 1538, together with the following crest: *On a chapeau vert doubled ermine a wyvern rising quarterly or and azure; mantling, gules doubled argent buttoned or.* In the arms granted to Lord Audley the tinctures and the martlets appear to have been derived from the coat of the Audleys of Essex: *Or, on a fess azure between three hares sable three martlets argent*; while the fret was taken from the arms of the Audleys who were powerful in the Western Marches in the fourteenth century: *Gules, a fret or.* While the eagles in his shield were not blazoned in detail, they were illustrated in the grant as displayed and having their wings inverted. In various representations of the arms used by the college, the wings are found sometimes inverted and sometimes expanded.

The grant of 1538 did not include supporters, but when Lord Audley became a Knight of the Garter in 1541 the arms placed on his stall-plate in St George's Chapel, Windsor, showed the shield supported by two red dog-like creatures, collared and chained, each having three gold rays springing from its head. In a painting in the college hall the creatures have tusks and pointed snouts, but this was not made until 1714. In a manuscript at the College of Arms (Press I 2) known as *Prince Arthur's Book* a representation of one of Lord

Audley's supporters is shown with only two gold rays issuing from its head. Other sketches show creatures, sometimes tusked, with two or three rays. The beasts have not been identified but, if the three rays (perhaps straight horns) of the Garter stall-plate be accepted as correct, they may be intended for tricorns – a term given in the *Oxford English Dictionary* for imaginary creatures with three horns.

A seventeenth-century carving of the founder's arms in the First Court of the college shows the shield within the Garter and supported by two lions couchant gardant. Here a blunder occurs in the shield, the palewise line of the quarterly field not being indented. Below the shield is the motto, GARDE TA FOY (Keep thy faith).

A small seal dating perhaps from the early seventeenth century bears the Audley arms as quoted at the head of this article with the same motto. The common seal of the college bears an escutcheon charged with a wyvern passant to the sinister.

The monastic hostel which preceded the college is commemorated in the First Court by two shields bearing the arms of Croyland Abbey: *Quarterly; 1 and 4, Gules, three flaying knives erect argent, handles or* (for ST BARTHOLOMEW); *2 and 3, Azure, three scourges or* (for ST GUTHLAC).

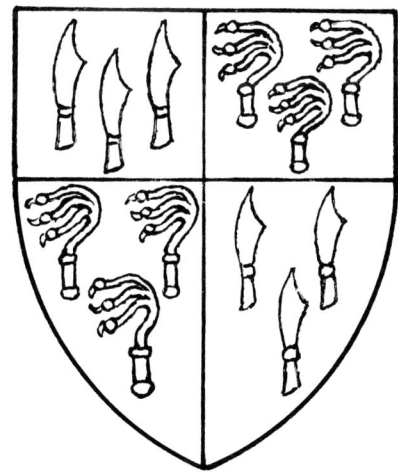

TRINITY COLLEGE

Arms

Argent, a chevron between three roses gules barbed
and seeded proper and on a chief gules a lion
passant gardant between two closed books all or.

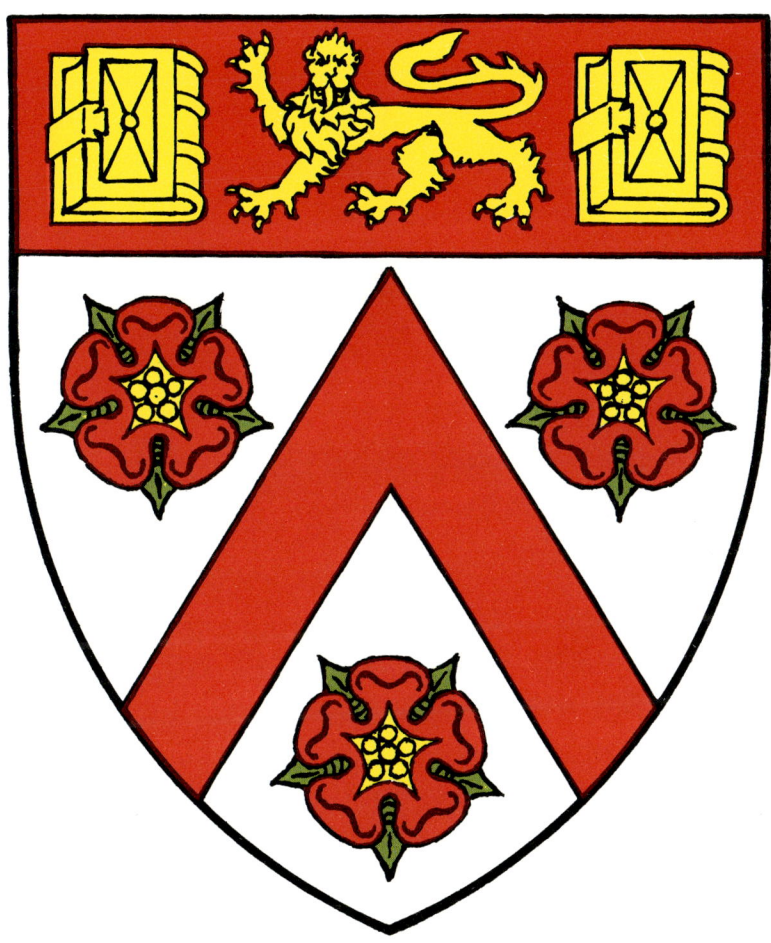

These arms were attributed to Trinity College in Parker's *Catalogus* (1572), and they were recorded as the arms of the college by Robert Cooke, Clarenceux King of Arms, at his Visitation in 1575. While no evidence of their having been formally granted exists, it is unlikely that Cooke would have recorded them unless some authority for their use had been produced at the Visitation. It is considered probable that a grant of arms was made to the college about the time of its foundation in 1546, and that this has been mislaid. At the 1648 Visitation the herald recorded merely 'arms as usual'.

The lion of England denotes the royal founder, King Henry VIII. The roses, also royal emblems, are three in number, doubtless with the intention of referring to the dedication of the college to the Holy and Undivided Trinity.

Henry created Trinity College by bringing together and enlarging two ancient foundations, Michaelhouse and King's Hall. 'The House of the Scholars of St Michael' had been founded in 1324 by Hervey de Stanton, Chancellor of the Exchequer to Edward II. On Hammond's map (1592), Michaelhouse is represented by the arms attributed to its founder: *Vair, a canton gules*. The seal of the foundation shows St Michael overcoming the dragon.

King's Hall had been founded in 1337 by Edward III in pursuance of a plan made by Edward II but not completed in his reign. In *The Book of Public*

Arms (1915) A.C. Fox–Davies gives for King's Hall, Cambridge: *Gules, three lions passant gardant in pale or within a bordure engrailed ermine*; but he adds that the arms are 'of no authority'. This coat differs only in the tincture of the border from that of Edward II's foundation of King's Hall, Oxford (now Oriel College), which has the border engrailed argent. It is a differenced form of the Royal Arms borne by Edward II, and by Edward III until 1340, when he quartered the ancient arms of France. The seal of King's Hall, Cambridge, shows Edward III seated under a canopy, holding a model of the hall and presenting the charter to the Master. A shield of the arms of England is to the left of the figure with the quartered arms of France Ancient and England to the right.

The shields of Michaelhouse and King's Hall appear on King Edward's Tower (1428–32, rebuilt 1600–1601), together with a roundel of England impaling France Ancient representing Edward II.

On the Great Gate, also a surviving portion of King's Hall, Edward III's arms (with the quarters for France) appear together with the arms of his six sons each with his appropriate label or border for difference, except for William of Hatfield who died too young to have arms assigned to him and is represented by a plain white shield.

In common with other colleges, Trinity is entitled to fly a banner of its arms. In practice, the flag which it uses is the banner of Edward III – *Quarterly France Ancient and England.*

EMMANUEL COLLEGE

Arms

As blazoned in the grant of 1588: Un Lyon Azur rampant en Champ D'argent Langué & Armé Gueule supportant en la patte dextre un Chappeau Triumphant de Laurier & sort de sa bouche ce Dicton EMMANVEL.

In modern blazon this is: Argent, a lion rampant azure langued and armed gules, holding in his dexter paw a wreath of laurel proper, and issuing from his mouth a scroll charged with the word EMMANUEL.

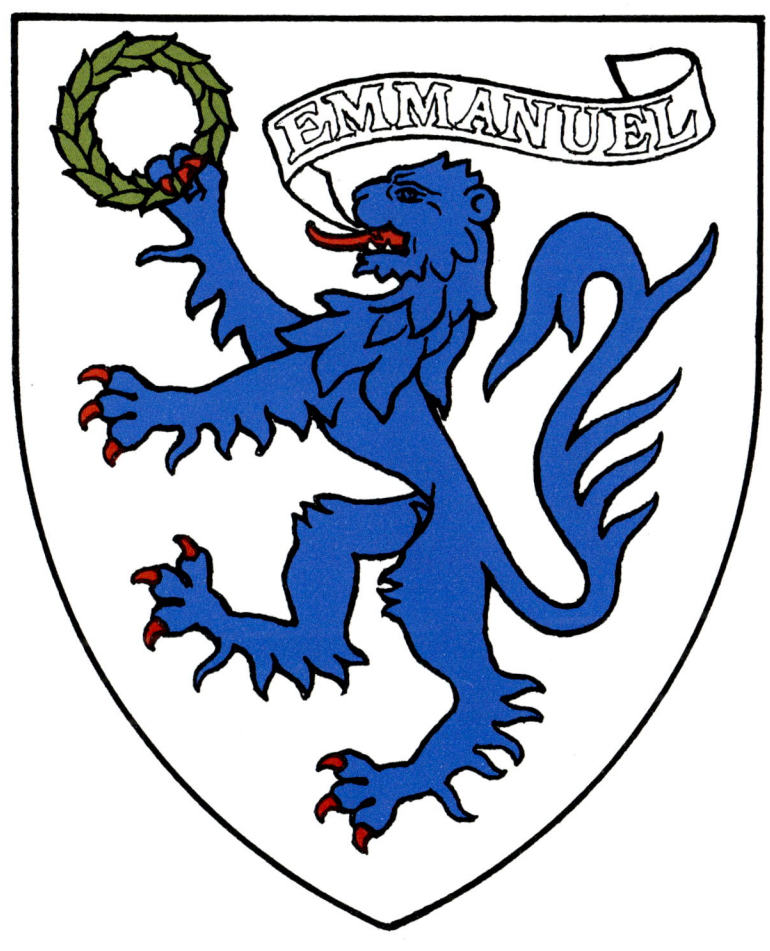

The tinctures of the scroll and the letters are not specified, but the marginal illustration on the patent shows the scroll white with black letters. In a book by John Scott of 1621 (C.U. Archive, Gg 5.21), it is black with yellow letters, and these are the tinctures in the college flag; but in modern representations of the arms it is usual to make the scroll blue with yellow or gold letters. A common error is failing to make the scroll come from the lion's mouth as the blazon requires.

The college arms appear on the common seal, but on the Master's seal they are treated as a crest and mounted on a crest-wreath.

Emmanuel College was founded by Sir Walter Mildmay on the site of a former house of Dominican friars. The Royal Charter was granted by Queen Elizabeth I on 11 January 1584 and the Deed of Foundation in the following May. The college was the first Protestant foundation in the University.

The arms were granted in 1588 by Robert Cooke, Clarenceux King of Arms, and the patent is preserved in the college library. The lion is taken from the 'ancient arms' of Mildmay allowed by Cooke to the founder on evidence now regarded as suspect.

Sir Walter, second son of Thomas Mildmay, a merchant of Chelmsford, was sometime Chancellor of the Exchequer. His elder brother Thomas obtained for their father a grant of arms: *Per fess nebuly argent and sable, three greyhounds' heads erased counterchanged collared gules.* These arms were used by Sir Walter in 1546, but in 1553 he obtained a new grant, *viz. Azure, on a bend argent a horse with wings courant sable langued gules.*

Thirty years later, in 1583, Sir Walter produced documents and seals to Robert Cooke, Clarenceux, in evidence of the right he claimed to the ancient arms said to have been used by his alleged ancestor, Henry de Mildmay of Stonehouse, Gloucestershire, in the time of Edward III and even by Henry's great-grandfather. Cooke accepted this evidence for the 'ancient arms': *3 lyons rampynge, which be azure in a feild silver, for none els in this land gyves the same: as by most diligent search made in y oldest and newest Recordes and Register of myne office is to be seene and prooved.* He also allowed that the 'newe' coat (the greyhounds' heads) should be quartered with the 'oulde'.

In the opinion of J. Horace Round, in 'The Mildmay Mystery', *Family Origins* (1930), Cooke was deceived by Mildmay. Gloucestershire histories make no mention of Mildmays at Stonehouse. The pedigree as registered by Cooke in 1583, and questioned by Round, is to be found in *Burke's Peerage* but expanded in G.E.C[ockayne] *Complete Peerage* (*sub* FitzWalter, vol. V, 1926) and *Complete Baronetage* (*sub* Mildmay, 1909).

SIDNEY SUSSEX COLLEGE

Arms
Argent, a bend engrailed sable [for RADCLIFFE]
impaling Or, a pheon azure [for SIDNEY].

These are the arms of the foundress, Lady Frances Sidney, Countess of Sussex, widow of Thomas Radcliffe, third Earl of Sussex. She died in 1589, making provision in her will for a new college at Cambridge, and in 1594 a Royal Charter was granted for the founding of a college. Building began in 1595, and 'the College of the Lady Frances Sidney Sussex' was formally constituted by the foundress's executors in February 1595–6, but the buildings were not ready for the reception of students until August 1598.

In a record of 'grantees of arms named in docquets and patents to the end of the seventeenth century' in the British Library (*Family History*, vol. 4, 1966, pp. 35ff.), it is stated that the above arms were granted to the college in 1675 by Sir Edward Walker, Garter King of Arms. In a seventeenth-century 'book of entrances' at the College of Arms the shields of Sidney and Radcliffe appear with the note, 'Sidney Sussex College bears these two impaled'. Walker's grant is not to be found among the Sidney muniments, nor is there an official record of it at the College of Arms. Nevertheless there is ample evidence that these have been regarded as the rightful arms of the college for 300 years.

The arms of the foundress were set up over the original gateway to the college in 1598. From Loggan's print (1688) it appears that these arms consisted of the coats of Radcliffe and Sidney impaled on a lozenge (the form appropriate to a widow), ensigned with the coronet of a countess, and supported on the dexter side by the bull of Radcliffe and on the sinister by the porcupine of Sidney. (The practice of taking the sinister supporter from the wife's paternal heraldry was not unusual at that time.) A similar achievement of arms was set up in the college hall about 1750, and another was incorporated in the war memorial in the ante-chapel in the present century.

The Master's seal also showed a lozenge ensigned with a coronet and bearing the foundress's paternal arms as they appear on her tomb in Westminster Abbey, i.e. the Sidney coat *quartering* Brandon, Clowfield, Barrington, Marcy, Mandeville, Chetwynd and Belhouse, with the motto, DIEU ME GARDE DE CALOMNIEZ (God preserve me from slanders). The achievement in the hall also has this motto. The corporate seal of the college bears the crests of Sidney and Radcliffe – a porcupine and an estoile.

In the corner of Loggan's print the college arms appear as Radcliffe impaling Sidney on a shield, the shield being the appropriate form for the arms of a corporate body, even though founded by a woman. No doubt if Walker's grant were found, it would show the arms on a shield. However, lacking the grant but possessing early instances of the foundress's arms on a lozenge ensigned by a coronet, the college has become accustomed to displaying the arms in this way, and they are so used on blazer badges, ties, etc. Strictly the arms on a lozenge ensigned by a coronet are commemorative of the foundress. The arms of the college as a corporate body should be placed on a shield, unaccompanied by a coronet or supporters.

DOWNING COLLEGE

Arms
Barry of eight argent and vert, a griffin segreant or within a bordure azure charged with eight roses of the first seeded and barbed proper.

Motto
QUAERERE VERUM

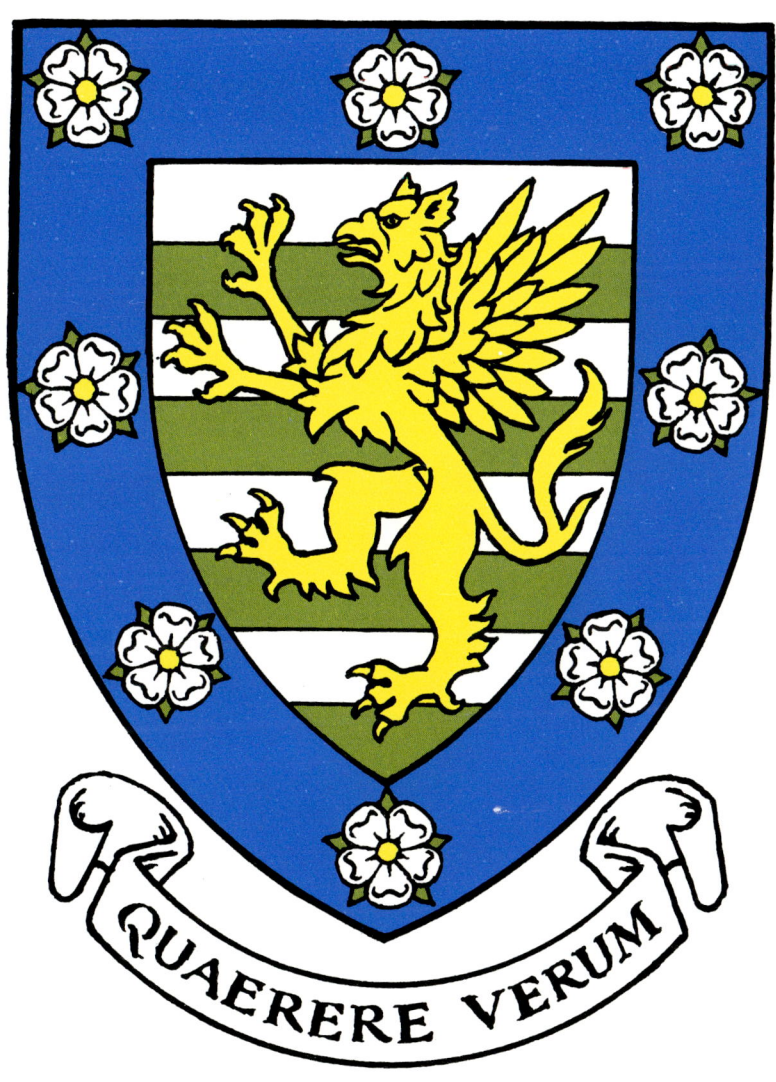

The foundation of Downing College in 1800 was the long-delayed consequence of the will of Sir George Downing, of Gamlingay Park, Cambridgeshire, third baronet, grandson of that George Downing whose ownership of a piece of land off Whitehall gave his name to one of the most famous streets in Britain. Sir George's will, dated 20 December 1717, directed that his extensive estates in Suffolk, Cambridge-shire and Bedfordshire were to pass to his nephew George Garrard Downing and his issue, with remainder to other relatives in a similar way. In the event of failure of such issue the trustees were directed 'to purchase some piece of land lying and being in the town of Cambridge proper and convenient for the building of a college, which college to be called Downing's College. And my will is that a charter royal be sued for and obtained for the founding and incorporating a body collegiate by that name.'

After Sir George's death in 1749 the will was proved and the estates passed to his cousin Jacob Garrard Downing, fourth baronet, who died without issue in 1764 having outlived all the other devisees of the original will. However, Sir Jacob's widow and her nephew refused to give up the estate, and so it was not until 22 September 1800, after litigation, that the charter for the college was obtained. Building began in 1807.

The arms blazoned at the head of this article were granted to the college in 1801 by Sir Isaac Heard, Garter King of Arms; Thomas Lock, Clarenceux; and George Harrison, Norroy. They consist of the arms of the founder differenced by a blue border with white roses. An examination of the arms used by members of the Downing family shows variations in the number of pieces forming the barry field. The arms of the first baronet at East Hatley church, Cambridgeshire, show barry of eight, while the seal of the third baronet displays barry of ten. Both forms are found in Burke's *Extinct Baronetcies* and *General Armory*. So far as Downing College is concerned, the Kings of Arms put the matter beyond doubt by granting barry of eight. The motto may be translated 'Search for the truth'.

GIRTON COLLEGE

Arms

Quarterly vert and argent, a cross flory
counterchanged between in the first and fourth
quarters a roundel ermine and in the second and
third quarters a crescent gules.

These arms were granted in 1928. They are composed of charges and tinctures selected from heraldic insignia associated with the four persons principally concerned in the foundation of the college, namely:

Mr H.R. Tomkinson, who bore: *Azure, a cross patonce between four martlets or, all within a bordure ermine.*

Madame Bodichon (née Leigh Smith): *Ermine, three roundels or* (for SMITH).

Henrietta Maria, Lady Stanley of Alderley (daughter of the thirteenth Viscount Dillon): *Argent, a lion passant between three crescents gules* (for DILLON).

Miss Emily Davies, who had no family arms but is represented by the Welsh colours, green and white.

In 1862, as part of the movement for the emancipation and education of women, a group which included Emily Davies and Mme Bodichon (formerly Barbara Leigh Smith) formed a committee to press for the admission of girls to the Oxford and Cambridge Local Examinations. They had the support of H.R. Tomkinson, a man of administrative and financial experience who included among his activities the secretaryship of the London centre of the Cambridge Local Examinations. Largely due to his advocacy the Cambridge Syndicate agreed to allow girls to sit for the examinations.

These three pioneers then joined with others in a project to found, by public subscription, a college for women, 'designed to hold, in relation to girls' schools and home teaching, a position analogous to that occupied by the universities towards public schools for boys'. An executive committee, with Miss Davies as secretary and Mr Tomkinson as a member, was formed to bring the college into being. In 1869 the college was established at Benslow House, Hitchin, with five students in the first year. Among those who held the position of Mistress in the early years were Mme Bodichon and Lady Stanley of Alderley, both of whom were also generous benefactors of the college after its removal to its present site.

The decision to transfer the college to the vicinity of Cambridge was taken in 1872 when land was acquired near the village of Girton and building was begun. The move to the new premises took place in October 1873, and from that time the establishment was named Girton College. Miss Davies was the Mistress at the time of the move.

Thereafter Girton College made steady progress in numbers, accommodation and scholarship. Originally incorporated as an association under the Board of Trade, its standing was enhanced, and its growing reputation recognised, by the grant of a Royal Charter in 1924.

In 1948, as a result of changes in the statutes of the University admitting women to equal membership, Girton attained the full status of a college of the University.

NEWNHAM COLLEGE

Arms

Argent, on a chevron azure between in chief two crosses botonny fitchy and in base a mullet sable, a griffin's head erased or between two mascles of the field.

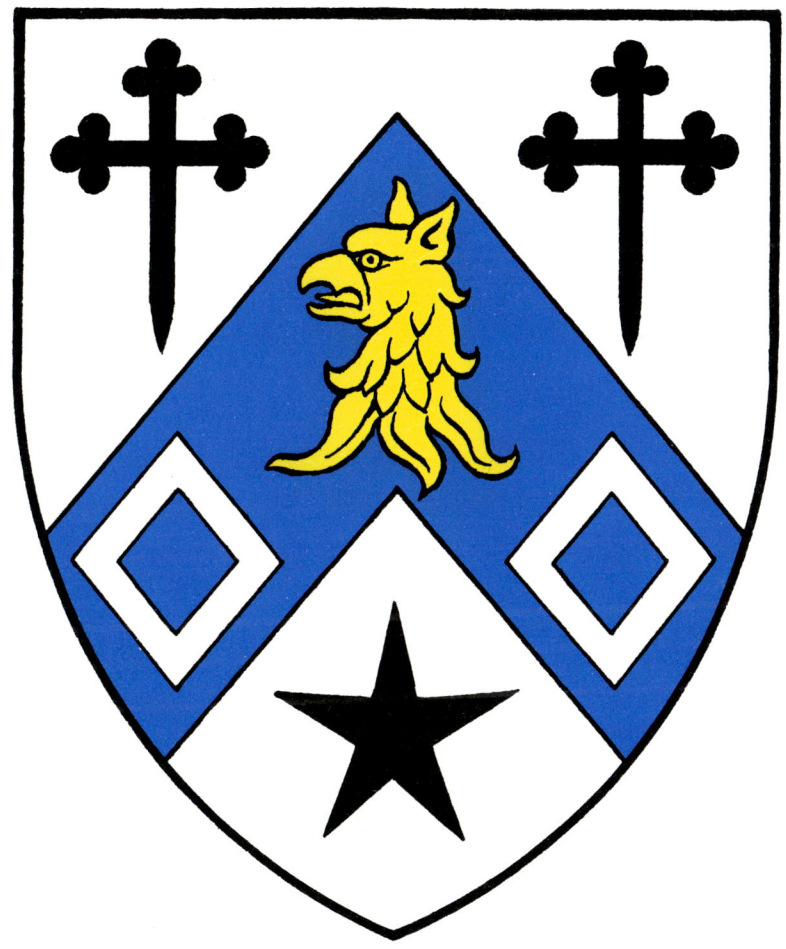

These arms, granted in 1923, were designed by the Revd E.E. Dorling to incorporate charges from the arms of those intimately connected with the founding of the college.

The history of Newnham begins with the formation of the Association for Promoting the Higher Education of Women in Cambridge, in 1869. A house of residence was opened in 1871 in Regent Street where there were five students under the care of Miss A.J. Clough. As the number grew, the community moved first to Merton Hall, then to premises in Bateman Street, and then with the foundation of the Newnham Hall Company in 1875 into what is now the Old Hall of Newnham College.

The college formally came into existence in 1880 with the amalgamation of the Association and the Company. Women were admitted to titles of degrees from 1881. In 1948 Newnham, like Girton, attained the full status of a college of the University.

In the early years of the college Miss A.J. Clough was the principal. She came of the family of Clough of Plas Clough, Denbighshire, which bore: *Azure, between three mascles a greyhound's head couped argent*. The out-students were under the care of Miss Marion Kennedy. She bore: *Argent, a chevron gules between in chief two crosses botonny fitchy sable and in base a boar's head couped sable langued gules* – a coat slightly differing from that of Kennedy of Kirkmichael, Ayrshire, which has crosses crosslet fitchy.

The other great benefactors of the college were Mr (later Professor) Henry Sidgwick, and Miss E.M. Balfour, whom he married in 1876. Mrs Sidgwick later became a principal of one of the halls of Newnham College. Their arms were – Sidgwick (assumed arms): *Gules, a fess between three griffins' heads erased or*; and Balfour (of Balbirnie): *Argent, on a chevron engrailed between three mullets sable an otter's head erased argent.*

In the college arms the chevron links them with the coats of Balfour and Kennedy, while its colour and the mascles refer to Clough. The crosses come from Kennedy, the mullet from Balfour, and the griffin's head from Sidgwick. No crest was granted, for although a corporate body may have a crest, it was thought that a crest and helm would be inappropriate to one composed entirely of women.

SELWYN COLLEGE

Arms

Per pale gules and argent, a cross potent quadrate argent and or between four crosses paty [correctly termed formy], those to the dexter argent, those to the sinister or [for the SEE of LICHFIELD] *impaling* Argent, on a bend cotised sable three annulets or [for SELWYN]; all within a bordure sable.

Crest

On a wreath argent and purpure, in front of a book erect bound gules, edged, clasped and garnished or, a representation of the pastoral staff of Bishop Selwyn; mantling purpure and argent.

Badge

A mitre or within an annulet purpure.

Motto

ΑΝΔΡΙΖΕΣΘΕ

ΑΝΔΡΙΖΕΣΘΕ

The college was founded by public subscription as a memorial to George Augustus Selwyn, Bishop of New Zealand and later Bishop of Lichfield until his death in 1878. It received a Royal Charter in 1882, but because the college's statutes restricted entry to members of the Church of England it was recognised only as a public hostel. It became an Approved Foundation in 1926 and, following a change in its statutes removing the restriction on entry, it attained full collegiate status in 1958. An anonymous donation by a former member enabled the college to petition for arms, and the armorial bearings blazoned above were granted in 1964.

Before obtaining the grant of arms the college had, from its foundation, made use of the arms borne by Bishop Selwyn as Bishop of Lichfield, which were incorrect in certain respects. In the Lichfield coat the half of the central cross and also the two crosses formy on the argent field were shown as red, whereas they should have been gold. This unusual feature of gold crosses on silver was derived from the arms of the kingdom of Jerusalem (see Queens' College), perhaps with reference to an early Bishop of Lichfield, Roger de Clinton, who took the cross and died at Antioch in 1148. The see has now reverted to this ancient form of its arms, which are properly shown in the dexter half of the college shield.

During the enquiries before the granting of arms it was found that Bishop Selwyn had used the arms of the wrong branch of the family. He bore the arms of Selwyn of Friston, Sussex: *Argent, on a bend cotised sable three annulets or within a bordure engrailed gules*; to which he added a *crescent gules for difference*, and this was the coat which appeared on the sinister side of the original shield of the college. The arms without the border were given in the 1682–3 Visitation of Gloucestershire for Selwyn of Horsemarley, Rodborough and Frampton, and the reprint of the published version of the heralds' record by Fitz-Roy Fenwick and Metcalfe traces the pedigree of the family down to Bishop Selwyn. Accordingly the Selwyn arms as granted to the college omit the red engrailed border, and also the crescent.

Permission to use the Lichfield and Selwyn coats was given by the Bishop of Lichfield and the head of the Selwyn family, and the impaled coats were granted within a bordure sable to difference the arms of the college from those of Bishop Selwyn.

The crest represents the original hardwood staff of Maori workmanship, with an inlaid mother-of-pearl cross, used by Bishop Selwyn as his pastoral staff in New Zealand and now in the possession of the college.

The motto, from the *First Epistle to the Corinthians* 16: 13, is inscribed over the gate of the college, and may be translated as 'Quit ye like men'.

FITZWILLIAM COLLEGE

Arms

Lozengy argent and gules, a chief of the arms of the
University of Cambridge.

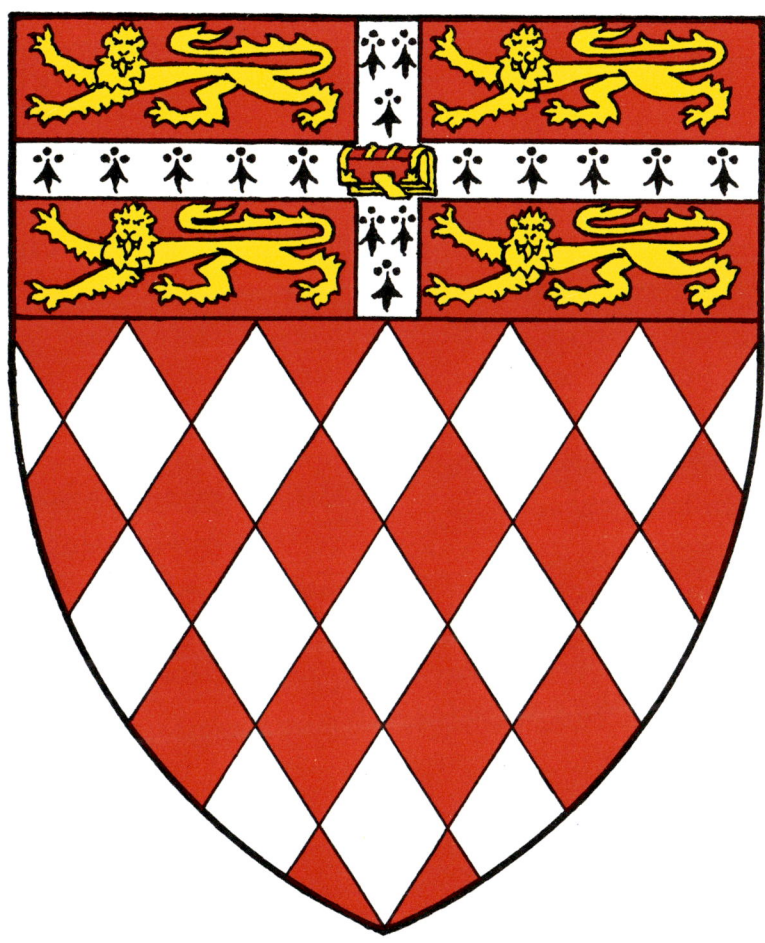

These arms were granted to the college in 1974, but for many years they had been used, without heraldic authority, by its predecessor, Fitzwilliam House, the organisation for non-collegiate students.

The University began to admit students not members of any college in 1869 and appointed a Board to regulate their affairs. In 1887 the Board acquired a house in Trumpington Street to serve as offices and a centre for the corporate activities developing among the students. The amalgamated clubs formed by the students, needing a name more evocative than 'non-collegiate', adopted 'Fitzwilliam' because their house was opposite the Fitzwilliam Museum and adjacent to Fitzwilliam Street. Thus the house, and the organisation occupying it, came to be called 'Fitzwilliam Hall' (later 'House') though it had no connection with the Museum or its founder, Richard, seventh Viscount Fitzwilliam of Meryon (1745–1816).

In 1887 the Fitzwilliam Boat Club, wishing for an heraldic device to paint on the bows of their boats, and for a boat flag (after the custom of the colleges) adopted a shield consisting of the Fitzwilliam arms as displayed in the Museum: *Lozengy argent and gules*, to which the club added a chief of the arms of the University. The Fitzwilliams of Meryon could not be consulted as their line had ceased in 1833, but the lozengy coat was also borne by the Earls Fitzwilliam, and the club obtained the permission of the sixth Earl to use his arms in this way. The use of this device spread from rowing to other activities, and it was eventually accepted by the University as the shield of Fitzwilliam House.

In 1966 Fitzwilliam House was incorporated by Royal Charter as Fitzwilliam College. Naturally the college wished to continue the use of the device which had been associated with its predecessor in name for eighty years, but the permission given by the sixth Earl did not constitute a sufficient connection with the Fitzwilliam family to justify the Kings of Arms in granting the lozengy coat to the college as part of an authorised shield of arms. However, a formal link between the family and the college was established when the present Earl Fitzwilliam accepted the position of Patron of the college. The Kings of Arms were then able to grant the college the arms of Fitzwilliam with those of the University of Cambridge in the chief.

CHURCHILL COLLEGE

Arms

Quarterly: 1 and 4, Sable, a lion rampant argent, on a canton of the last a cross gules; 2 and 3, Quarterly argent and gules, in the second and third quarters a fret or, on a bend sable three escallops also argent; over all in the fess point an open book likewise argent.

Crest

On a wreath of the colours, a lion couchant gardant argent supporting with the dexter forepaw a staff or, flying therefrom a banner gules charged with an open book also argent.

Motto
FORWARD

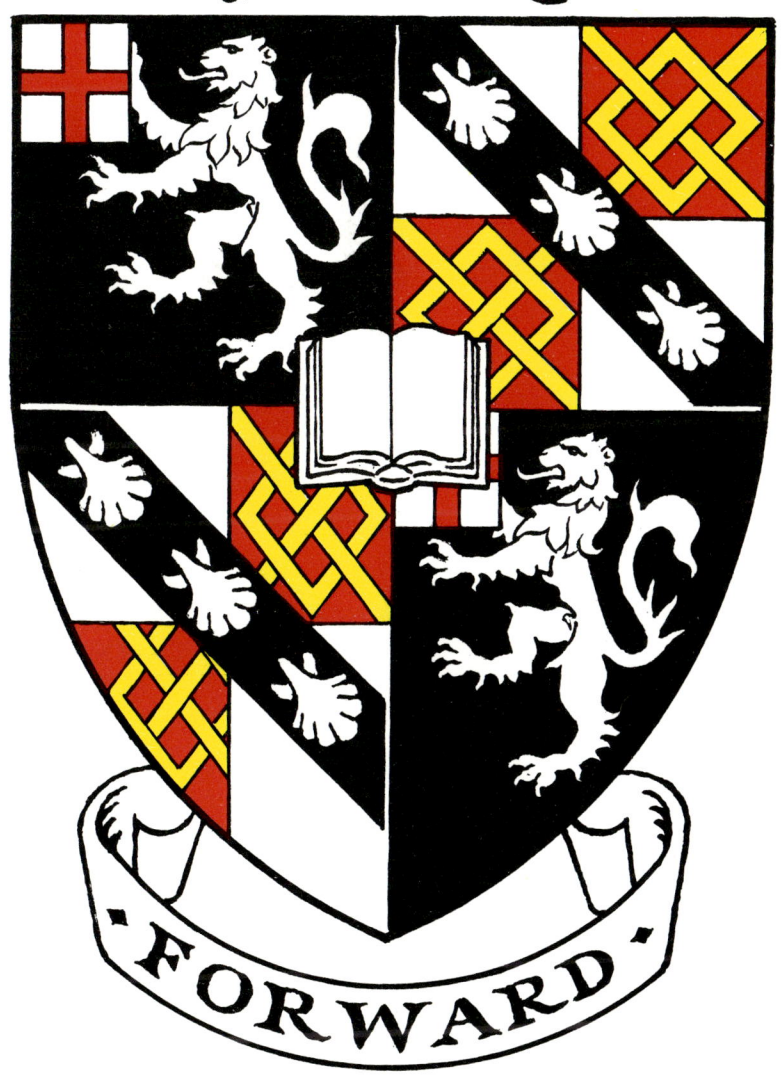

FORWARD

These armorial bearings were granted in 1959 to be borne by the Trustees of the Churchill College Trust and by the Master, Fellows and Scholars of their proposed college at Cambridge by whatsoever name it should be incorporated. The arms are the quarterly coats of Churchill and Spencer with an open book over all for difference, while the crest is that of Churchill also differenced with a book.

The Churchill College Trust was set up in 1958 under the chairmanship of the Right Hon. Sir Winston Leonard Spencer-Churchill, K.G., O.M., C.H., for the purpose of founding a new college at Cambridge honouring Sir Winston 'as a memorial'. The college admitted the first post-graduates in 1960 and the first undergraduates in the following year.

The first Sir Winston Churchill (d. 1688) bore: *Sable, a lion rampant argent, over all a bendlet gules.* At the Restoration, for his loyal service to Charles II, he was granted as an augmentation to his arms *a canton argent charged with the cross of St George gules.* The augmentation in itself being a sufficient difference, he discontinued the use of the bendlet. His arms passed to his son, John Churchill, who became the first Duke of Marlborough, and to John's eldest daughter, Henrietta, who succeeded as Duchess of Marlborough but whose only son died without issue. At Henrietta's death the honours devolved upon the son of her younger sister Anne who had married

Charles Spencer, third Earl of Sunderland, and the fifth Earl succeeded as Duke of Marlborough and quartered the coats of Churchill and Spencer. To these were added, as an augmentation commemorating the victories of the first Duke, *an escutcheon argent charged with the cross of St George gules, and thereon an escutcheon of the arms of France – Azure, three fleurs-de-lis or.* The arms thus augmented descended to Sir Winston Churchill together with the Churchill crest of *a lion couchant gardant argent supporting a banner gules charged with a dexter hand argent.*

When the question of arms for Churchill College was under consideration, Sir George Bellew, Garter, agreed that the arms and crest of Sir Winston might be granted to the college, omitting the augmentation and differencing the shield with an open book argent, and substituting a similar book for the hand in the crest. This was approved first by Sir Winston and then by the other trustees. The motto, FORWARD, was Sir Winston's personal choice.

Mr H.H. Corson, of Nashville, Tennessee, whose gift enabled the college to obtain a grant of armorial bearings, considered that having arms would help fund-raising in the United States.

The arms appear on the college seal.

NEW HALL

Arms

Sable, a dolphin palewise, head downwards to the
dexter, in chief three mullets fesswise, a bordure
embattled argent.

New Hall was established in 1954
by the Association to Promote a Third Foundation for Women in the
University of Cambridge. The arms were granted in 1971. Full collegiate
status was achieved in 1972.

When the design of the arms was under consideration the fellows
expressed the wish that the principal charge should be a dolphin – a creature
noted for its intelligence and for forming social groups termed 'schools', and
traditionally well disposed to humankind. It was also taken as symbolising
the River Cam, while the embattled border alludes to the college's situation
overlooking the site of Cambridge castle and the Roman town. The three
mullets are from the arms of Murray, with reference to Miss A.R. Murray,
later Dame Rosemary Murray, first President of New Hall (and, 1975–1977,
the first woman Vice-Chancellor in the University's history).

DARWIN COLLEGE

Arms

Argent, on a bend gules cotised vert between two mullets each within an annulet gules three escallops or [for DARWIN] *impaling* Per fess dancetty azure and gules, a caduceus between in chief two roses or [for RAYNE]; all within a bordure or.

Crest

On a wreath or and azure, in front of a lion passant or murally crowned azure, holding in the dexter forepaw a key wards outward or, three escallops argent.

Badge

A leading rein interlaced azure, the clip to the dexter, entwining an escallop or.

These arms were granted in 1966.

Darwin College was founded in 1964 by a trust consisting of members of Gonville and Caius, St John's, and Trinity Colleges. The first graduate college established in modern times, it was formed to meet the rapid expansion in the number of research students and University teaching officers for whom the existing colleges could not make adequate provision. In January 1965, following adjustment of the University statutes to include graduate colleges, Darwin became an Approved Foundation in the University, and in 1976 a full college.

The armorial bearings commemorate the principal benefactors of the foundation – the Darwin family and Sir Max Rayne. On the death of Sir Charles Galton Darwin, K.B.E., F.R.S., in 1962, his widow and remaining family decided to vacate their Cambridge home, Newnham Grange, and agreed that it should be acquired for the projected graduate college, and that this should bear the name 'Darwin'. Sir Charles's brother, Mr Reginald Darwin, and other members of the family became liberal benefactors of the college. In addition, the Max Rayne Foundation provided the college with a large endowment, while Sir Max Rayne made a generous personal contribution.

When arms were devised for the college it was considered appropriate that they should consist of the coats of Darwin and Rayne joined by impalement within a border – an arrangement like that already used in the case of Gonville and Caius College. The arms of Darwin, as borne by the college, were granted in 1890 to Reginald Darwin of Fern, Derbyshire, to be borne by the descendants of his father and uncle, the latter being the great-grandfather of Sir Charles Darwin of Newnham Grange. The arms of Sir Max Rayne were granted in 1963.

The badge consists of an escallop from the Darwin coat entwined by a rein allusive to Rayne.

WOLFSON COLLEGE

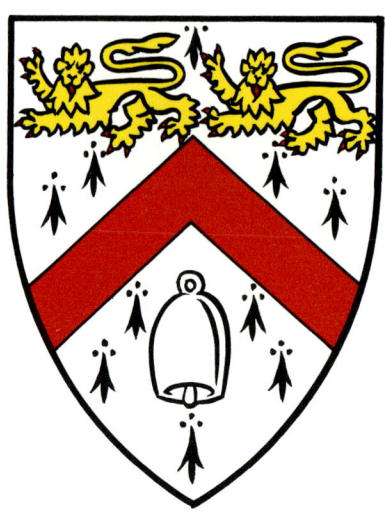

Arms
Ermine, a chevron gules between in chief two lions passant gardant or and in base a handbell proper.

Crest
On a wreath argent and gules, a demi lion or holding in its dexter paw a handbell proper.

Motto
RING TRUE

B y the late 1950s it had become embarrassingly apparent that many of the university's facilities, departments and administrative bodies, and some independent Cambridge organisations with strong academic links, had increased greatly in size and importance but that a growing proportion of their graduate members had little involvement or none in the colleges. The University therefore appointed a syndicate under the chairmanship of Lord Bridges to enquire into the relationship between the University and the colleges.

One important consequence of this enquiry was the starting in 1965 of a new graduate college founded by the University itself, and therefore named University College. It was open to senior graduates and graduate students of either sex.

In recognition of a major benefaction by the Wolfson Foundation, which provided both permanent buildings and capital endowment, the present name was adopted in 1973; and armorial bearings were applied for commemorating the Wolfson family with the bell from their arms.

The chevron recalls the symbol formerly used on ties worn by members of University College, the lions and ermine being taken from the arms of the University itself in commemoration of the original foundation.

CLARE HALL

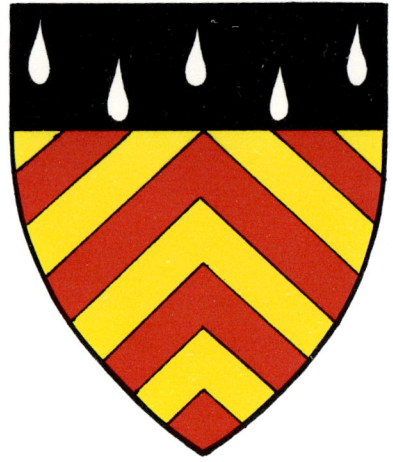

Arms

Chevronny or and gules, on a chief sable five
gouttes three and two argent.

When the report of Lord Bridges' syndicate on the relationship between the University and the colleges (*C.U. Reporter*, 1961–62, pp. 1073–1150) was discussed in Clare College, the first proposal was for a large increase in the size of the fellowship; but then it seemed better to found a new society that would differ from the parent body in aims and composition.

Out of these discussions arose the founding, under a Trust Deed dated 7 February 1966, of Clare Hall, a separate college, limited to established graduate scholars and graduate students, open to both sexes, and with a strong contingent of visiting fellows from other universities and countries.

The new college, endowed jointly by Clare College and the Ford Foundation and the Old Dominion Foundation, became an Approved Foundation of the University in 1966 and received its Royal Charter in 1984. The arms both reflect the relationship with the parent foundation, Clare College, and follow the family's ancient practice of varying the number of chevrons. A heraldic badge is being designed.

HUGHES HALL

Arms

Per fess gules and ermine, a pale counterchanged in the gules in chief two owls the dexter contourny and in base a torch erect or enflamed proper and for the Crest upon a helm with a wreath argent and azure Out of a garland of laurel leaves or two pairs of ostrich feathers erect azure quilled and banded with a ribbon tied on a bow argent.

Founded in 1885 as the Cambridge Training College for Women, all graduates, in 1949 it became a Recognised Institution of the University, and the following year the name was changed to Elizabeth Phillips Hughes Hall in honour of its first principal. In 1968 the Hall became an Approved Society. Rapid changes followed, bringing in subjects other than education, and research students were admitted. In 1971, the first fellows were elected. Men were admitted from 1973. Today about one fifth of the students are from overseas.

In the arms, granted in 1980, there is a combination of traditional symbols of education on a pleasingly composed field.

St Edmund's House

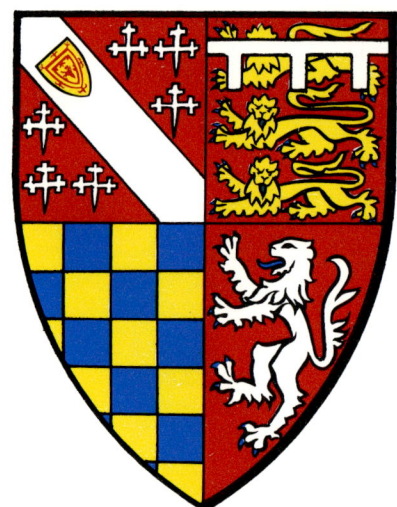

The house derives its origins from an academic community founded by Catholic emigrés from Oxford and Cambridge in 1568 at the University of Douai, and known as the English College. It continued in existence for nearly two and a half centuries and was then dispersed by the French Revolution. Some of the students reassembled in Hertfordshire to form St Edmund's College, Old Hall Green. A century later (1896) this college sent a colony of its students to resume university life in Cambridge, and the fifteenth Duke of Norfolk presented them with the property now known as St Edmund's House. In 1965 it was recognised by the University as an Approved Society and in 1975 as an Approved Foundation.

St Edmund's House has not obtained armorial bearings but its seal has heraldic features. This shows the figure of St Edmund de Abbendon, Archbishop of Canterbury 1233–40, wearing mitre and pallium and seated under a canopy with an open book on his knees and a cross in his right hand. The inscription, S. COMMUNE DOMUS SANCTI EDMUNDI CANTABRIGIAE, is interrupted on each side by a shield. The dexter bears the arms of the dukes of Norfolk, *Quarterly: 1, [Gules], a bend between six*

Arms of the
dukes of Norfolk

crosses crosslet fitchy [argent], on the bend an inescutcheon [or] charged with a demi lion within a double tressure pierced through the mouth with an arrow [all gules] (for HOWARD); *2, England with a label [argent] for difference* (for BROTHERTON); *3, Chequy [or and azure]* (for WARREN); *4, [Gules], a lion rampant [argent]* (for FITZALAN). The sinister bears *a cross patonce between four martlets.*

The latter coat is no doubt intended to represent St Edmund. The son of Edmund Rich, a merchant of Abingdon, he does not appear to have inherited arms, and there is no evidence that he bore arms during his lifetime. Nevertheless at a later date arms were assigned to him, apparently based on those of the Abbey of Abingdon. The arms of the Abbey were: *Argent, a cross patonce between four martlets sable.* In a series of shields of former archbishops painted in 1597 on the walls of the chapter house at Canterbury the arms attributed to St Edmund de Abbendon were: *Gules, a cross patonce or between four sea-pies sable winged argent.*

While the college retains its Roman Catholic tradition in membership and in worship, its character has been widened progressively in recent years: it welcomes people, including visiting scholars, with diverse attitudes to religion and from many countries, and has admitted women since 1972. Membership has been limited to about fifty, in order to retain close contact between fellows and members. The day-to-day running of the college is conducted by a council of the Master and fellows, who represent a wide range of disciplines within the University.

LUCY CAVENDISH COLLEGE

Arms

Per fess enarched azure and sable, in chief two bars wavy argent, over all issuant from the fess line a water lily also argent slipped and leaved vert, and in base a buck's head caboshed, between the attires a lozenge argent charged with an escallop sable.

Crest

On a wreath argent and azure, within a circlet azure charged with a barrulet argent and over all four estoiles or, a nautilus proper.

Lucy Caroline Cavendish (1841–1925), after whom the college is named, was a daughter of the fourth Lord Lyttelton, and the wife of Lord Frederick Charles Cavendish, M.P. The latter's family was connected with Cambridge, both the seventh and eighth Dukes of Devonshire having been Chancellors of the University, while the seventh also founded the Cavendish Laboratory. Lord Frederick, when Chief Secretary for Ireland, was murdered in Phoenix Park, Dublin.

Throughout her life Lucy Cavendish showed a strong interest in the education of women. She was appointed to the Royal Commission on Secondary Education in 1894, and among the causes she promoted was the Girls' Public Day School Trust.

Lucy Cavendish College, the fourth college for women in the University of Cambridge, became an Approved Society in 1965 after fourteen years of unofficial existence, and has now, in 1984, become an Approved Foundation. It originated with a group of women graduates involved in University affairs but not then closely attached to any college, who were especially concerned to help and encourage married women and others to return to academic or professional life after a period devoted to family or other commitments. In addition to the fellowship, the college now has a number of graduate students and mature undergraduates (those over twenty-five years of age).

The armorial bearings were granted to the college in 1973. The water lily was chosen as a floral emblem suited to a riverside situation, while the black part of the shield suggests the fenland soil. The buck's head on a black ground is from the arms of the Cavendish family, and the scallop shell is from the heraldry of the Lytteltons. In the crest the estoiles are 'lights' alluding to the name 'Lucy', and the nautilus was suggested by the work in the field of marine biology undertaken by Dr Anna Bidder, first principal of the college.

HOMERTON COLLEGE

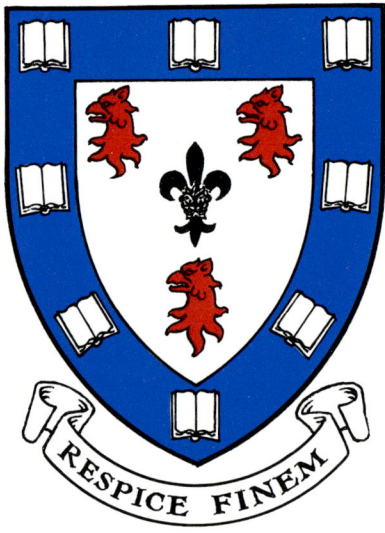

Arms
Argent, a leopard's face jessant-de-lis sable between three griffins' heads erased gules, on a bordure azure eight open books proper.

Crest
On a wreath of the colours, a demi griffin holding between the claws a lozenge argent charged with a leopard's face jessant-de-lis as in the Arms.

Motto
RESPICE FINEM

In 1768 at the then pleasant village of Homerton, adjoining the London suburb of Hackney, a Congregationalist academy was established, and in 1825 it was extended and named 'Homerton College'. Its role was changed in 1849 to that of training teachers, both men and women. The Congregational Board of Education decided to move the college out of London, and in 1893 took a tenancy of the buildings of the former Cavendish College in Hills Road, Cambridge. In the following year it was decided to admit no more men. In 1977 Homerton was recognised by the University as an Approved Society, which now, once more, admits men.

The first move to adopt heraldic insignia came in 1894 when the Congregational Board of Education asked George Unwin, one of its members, 'to secure the arms of Mr Morley and Mr Baines, as the founders of the college, as a basis'. Three generations of the Morley family (the stocking knitters) were closely connected with the college as Treasurers of the Society, and Samuel Morley was also Treasurer of the Congregational Board of Education. The Morley arms were: *Argent, a leopard's face jessant-de-lis sable between three griffins' heads erased gules*. Baines, a former member of the Board, was found not to have had arms. Accordingly a shield was devised consisting of the three griffins' heads from the Morley coat impaling the arms of Jennings (another family long connected with the Board): *A chevron between three plummets*; and to these was added a chief charged with three fleurs-de-lis from the arms of Unwin, for the first principal of that name. The result, in the words of the college history, could be blazoned: *Argent, three griffins' heads erased azure,* impaling *Argent, a chevron between three plummets azure; on a chief of light azure three fleurs-de-lis azure.* The shield was surmounted by a laurel chaplet, the badge of the old college at Homerton, and later the motto, RESPICE FINEM, was added.

In 1954 the grant of armorial bearings was obtained from the Kings of Arms. The Morley family coat was placed on the shield and differenced with a *bordure azure charged with eight open books* as symbols of learning. The crest was also based on that of Morley, but the leopard's face was placed on a lozenge, because then the college was for women only.

ROBINSON COLLEGE

Arms

Azure, in base two bars wavy argent over all a
Pegasus rampant or gorged with a crown rayonny
gules.

Robinson College was the first in
either of the ancient English universities to have been intended, from its
foundation, for both graduate and undergraduate students, of either sex. It
became a constituent part of the University as an Approved Foundation in
1977, and was granted its Royal Charter in 1985.

The college owes its existence to the munificence of a son of the City
of Cambridge, Mr David Robinson (b.1904), long famed for his many
philanthropic acts outside the University as well. He was knighted in 1985.

The founder's love of the river and abiding interest in horse racing are
neatly shown in the college arms by the winged horse Pegasus over the wavy
bars.

RIDLEY HALL

Arms
Party per pale gules and argent, on the dexter two swords in saltire points upwards proper, hilt and pommel or, and on the sinister in chief a bull passant of the first and in base a rush plant flowered and eradicated also proper, the whole within a bordure ermine.

Crest
On a wreath of the colours, a bishop's mitre between two slips of bulrush proper.

Motto
MARTYRII MEMORES

The armorial bearings were granted in 1952, and were based upon a shield in use before that date showing the arms of the See of London impaling those attributed to Bishop Ridley.

Ridley Hall was founded in 1879 as the product of a movement among evangelicals in the Church of England which was concerned to provide graduate ordinands of Oxford and Cambridge with a training in theology, preaching and pastoral work. It took its name from Nicholas Ridley, Bishop of London, sometime Master of Pembroke Hall, Cambridge, who with Hooper, Latimer and Cranmer, was burned at the stake at Oxford in 1555.

At the College of Arms there is no record that Bishop Ridley bore arms, but there is an entry dated 1581 that one Thomas Ridley, of Willimontswick, Northumberland, obtained confirmation of his 'ancient arms', these being: *Argent, a bull gules passant through reeds.* This coat appears on a portrait of Bishop Ridley dated 1555 in the National Portrait Gallery. Another portrait of the same date in the Master's lodge at Pembroke College shows the bull statant on more solid yet rough ground.

In the arms placed on the tower of Ridley Hall, and apparently based on a shield in the hall at Pembroke dating from its rebuilding in 1875, the Ridley coat is shown with a clear division between the bull and the reeds, as if the field were party per fess, and the reeds appear more like flowers. This form was used by stationers and others producing articles bearing the arms. G.K. Beaulah, in *Scholastic Arms* (1936), blazoned and illustrated the Ridley half of the shield as: *Vert, semy of flowers gentle, on a chief argent an ox gules.*

To settle the question of the correct form of the arms, in 1939 Dr F. W. Bullock, who had been Vice-Principal of the college, 1931–36, offered to defray the cost of a grant by the Kings of Arms. This was gratefully accepted by the Council, but owing to the outbreak of war the matter had to be deferred, and it was reopened with the College of Arms in 1952. Dr Bullock had asked that the new arms should be as similar as possible to the shield in former use, and though an identical coat could not be granted changes were kept to a minimum. The flowers in the lower part of the Ridley coat were replaced by *a rush plant flowered and eradicated proper*; and so that they might be seen against their background, they, like the bull, were placed on a field argent. To distinguish the arms of the Hall from those of the Bishop, the impaled coats of the See of London and Ridley were placed within an ermine border. The Hall had formerly placed a mitre above the shield, but as this was permissible only to a bishop it was replaced by a crest consisting of a mitre between two slips of bulrush. The motto was chosen by the Council.

To complete the account of the Ridley Hall heraldry it must be mentioned that the arms on the 1912 building are erroneous. They consist of the coat of the See of London impaling: *On a chevron between three hawks three roundels*. These are the arms given for Bishop Ridley in his biography by Gloster Ridley (1763) and in Burke's *General Armory*, but researches by Aubrey Toppin, late Norroy and Ulster King of Arms, showed that there was no evidence that these arms were used by any members of the Ridley family before 1628.

WESTCOTT HOUSE

Arms

Of Brooke Foss Westcott, Bishop of Durham:
Azure, a cross or between four lions rampant argent
[for the SEE of DURHAM] *impaling*, Argent, a
bend cotised sable within a bordure engrailed gules
bezanty [for WESTCOTT].

Westcott House originated in a scheme for providing theological training for undergraduates and graduates of the University intending to offer themselves for the ministry of the Church of England, which first found expression in the Cambridge Clergy Training School launched in 1881.

Brooke Foss Westcott, Regius Professor of Divinity, was the prime mover. He served as Chairman of the Council from 1881 to 1889, then becoming Bishop of Durham. He dedicated its first block of buildings in 1899 and after his death in 1901 the school changed its name to Westcott House.

Bishop Westcott used the arms assumed by his great-grandfather, Foss Westcott, a successful East India Company merchant, after his return from India in 1757. These were the arms of the Devonshire family of Westcote. They may be seen in a memorial window to Bishop Westcott in All Saints' church, Cambridge.

Westcott House makes no claim to arms, but it places the impaled coats blazoned above on its seal as the arms of its founder.

THE WESTMINSTER AND CHESHUNT COLLEGES

Westminster College and Cheshunt College were separate Nonconformist foundations. Until recent years each had its own buildings and establishment, but in 1965, for economic reasons and in accordance with the principle of ecumenical training for the Christian ministry, the colleges decided to work more closely together, sharing one building and developing a joint curriculum. The two colleges, which are required by their trust deeds to retain their separate legal identities, are now known by the joint name, The Westminster and Cheshunt Colleges.

Westminster College

Westminster College has no arms but uses a device consisting of a wreath of palm and thereon an open book inscribed: THE WORD OF GOD. This is usually found on an oval (as on the seal) within the inscription, COLL. WESTMONASTERIENSE APUD CANTABRIGIAM.

One of the first consequences of the formation of a separate jurisdiction for members of the Church of Scotland resident in England was the foundation of a Presbyterian theological college in London in 1844. After long consideration, it was decided in 1895 to move the college to Cambridge. The memorial stone of the new building was laid in 1897, and the name 'Westminster College' was chosen in commemoration of the Westminster Assembly of Divines, 1643–9.

Among Presbyterian churches the adoption of distinctive insignia is traditional, and a large number of such insignia, from many parts of the world, are displayed in the plaster of the ceiling of Westminster College hall. The college followed this tradition in developing its own device.

Since 1690 the Church of Scotland has used the emblem of a burning bush (also used by the French Reformed Church since 1583) with the motto, NEC TAMEN CONSUMEBATUR (Yet not burned, *Exodus* 3: 2). This device was placed on an English rose by the Presbyterian Church in England which achieved independence in 1844. Two groups which had earlier seceded from the Church of Scotland combined in 1847 to form the United Presbyterian Church, which had as its insignia, on a wreath of palm an open book inscribed: THE WORD OF THE LORD ENDURETH FOR EVER. At the union of these two churches in 1876 the two emblems were placed side by side in two intersecting circles, with the dove with outstretched wings symbolic of the Holy Spirit presiding over the union. In addition, the united church – the Presbyterian Church of England – adopted the motto, THIS IS THE WORD WHICH BY THE GOSPEL IS PREACHED UNTO YOU.

The college does not seem to have used any device before its move to

Cambridge. After the move they adopted one based on (and simplified from) that of the old United Presbyterian Church: an open book on a wreath, with the inscription THE WORD OF GOD.

Cheshunt College

In 1768 Selina, Dowager Countess of Huntingdon, founded a college at Trefecca, Breconshire, for the training of ministers to serve in the various chapels established by her. These were later obliged to secede from the Church of England, and became known as 'the Countess of Huntingdon's Connexion'. In 1792 it was removed to Cheshunt and took the name 'Cheshunt College', and in 1905 it was reorganised and moved to Cambridge. It is now associated with Westminster College in the manner described above.

The foundress was daughter and coheiress of Washington Shirley, Earl Ferrers, and widow of Theophilus Hastings, ninth Earl of Huntingdon. She bore arms based upon those of her husband and of her father, *viz. Quarterly, 1, Argent, a maunch sable* (for HASTINGS); *2, Quarterly France and England, a label of three points argent each charged with a canton gules* (for GEORGE, DUKE of CLARENCE); *3, Per pale or and sable, a saltire engrailed counter-changed* (for DE LA POLE); *4, Sable, two bars and in chief three roundels argent* (for HUNGERFORD); *and on an escutcheon of pretence her paternal arms, Quarterly, Paly of six or and azure, a canton ermine* (for SHIRLEY) *and England, a bordure argent* (for THOMAS of WOODSTOCK).

The earliest known use of these arms by the college was on the cover of the annual report in 1827. Here the arms were placed on a lozenge (appropriate to a widow) ensigned with a countess's coronet and supported on the dexter side by a man-tiger, one of the Earl of Huntingdon's supporters, and on the sinister by an ermine talbot for Shirley, Earl Ferrers. Man-tigers appeared as lions with human faces. The ermine dogs had red ears and coronet collars of gold. The motto below the supported lozenge was IN VERITATE VICTORIA (Victory in truth). The Countess's achievement in this form was placed on the gatehouse of the college buildings in Cambridge.

WESLEY HOUSE

Arms

Gules, a cross between four escallops or, on a chief sable an open book leaved argent, edged and clasped gold.

Motto

LUX VITA CARITAS

These arms were granted in 1926.

Wesley House was founded as the result of a decision by a number of leading Methodists to make a return to one of the old universities, from which Nonconformists had long been excluded, by establishing a college to prepare candidates for the Wesleyan Methodist ministry. Cambridge was chosen, because, in the words of the Revd G.S. Wakefield, 'the existence of the Leys School, founded in 1875, had done much to give Methodism scholarly status in the university town'.

In 1920 a trust fund was instituted, and in the Michaelmas term 1921 Wesley House opened its doors to the first six students. The college buildings, begun in 1923, were completed by 1930.

Wesley House was the first Cambridge theological college to receive a grant of arms. The cross and scallop shells are from a Wesley family coat, to which has been added the book on a black chief. The motto was chosen by the college (Light, Life, Love).

THE PERSE SCHOOL

Arms

Sable, a chevron ermine between three dragons'
heads erased argent.

Crest

On a wreath argent and sable, a pelican argent
membered sable vulning itself proper.

Motto

QUI FACIT PER ALIUM FACIT PER SE

The Perse School, for boys, was founded under the terms of the will of Dr Stephen Perse, Senior Fellow of Gonville and Caius College, who died in 1615. After Stephen's death his kinsman Martin Perse, of the Northwold branch of the family, became his principal trustee, and acquiesced in the use of the family arms over Stephen's tomb, although Stephen himself was not armigerous. These arms were adopted by the school. They are shown in the Visitation of Norfolk, 1563, as blazoned *Sable, a chevron ermine between three dragons' heads erased argent* and the crest as *a pelican argent membered sable vulning itself proper*. Several variations have been noted. According to S.J.D. Mitchell's *Perse: A History of the Perse School, 1615–1976*, there are obvious canting allusions. The pierced breast of the pelican alludes to the name Perse, and the sable of the field may be the nearest the heralds could get to the very dark blue used as 'perse' in French heraldry. The punning motto, *Qui facit per alium facit per se*, different from that used by the family – 'En Dieu est ma fiance' – splendidly reminds us of the work that Stephen wrought at the hands of Martin. For, if Stephen was the school's principal begetter, Martin was the conscientious guardian of its early fortunes.

On 1 February 1878 'the Governors of the Perse School resolved to raise the fees of the boys, in order to provide £150 per annum in aid of the Secondary Education of Girls . . .'. The Perse School for Girls opened on 17 January 1881 at 68 Trumpington Street. In 1883 the school was moved to its present principal site, in Panton Street. Today there are about 700 pupils. The link with the boys' school continues, three of the Governors serving also as Governors of the girls' school.

The Perse School for Girls, having no arms of its own, uses the pelican crest as it appears on Stephen's tomb but sable.

THE LEYS SCHOOL

Arms

Or, a cross gules charged in the centre with a mullet of the field, on a chief ermine an open book argent embellished of the first between two roses of the second, barbed and seeded proper.

Crest

On a wreath of the colours, a wyvern proper resting the dexter claw on an antique lamp or, flaming gules.

Motto

IN FIDE FIDUCIA

Opened in 1875 with sixteen boys, the Leys was the first Methodist public school.

The armorial bearings were granted in 1914 on the occasion of King George V's visit to the school to inaugurate the new library block. An unofficial device on an ornate shield had been in use since 1876.

The cross is symbolic of a Christian foundation, the book and the lamp are for learning, and the mullet (or star) is for scholastic merit and encouragement. Red roses may have been chosen because several of the founders were from Lancashire. The wyvern is the crest of the Wesley family. The motto proclaims 'Faithfulness in the faith'.

GLOSSARY

This glossary explains the heraldic terms used in this book.

The heraldic tinctures are as follows:

Metals
   Argent silver or white
   Or gold or yellow
Colours
   Azure blue
   Gules red
   Purpure purple
   Sable black
   Vert green
Furs
   Ermine white with black tufts
   Ermines in early heraldry an alternative spelling of *ermine*; later, the reverse of ermine, i.e. black with white tufts
   Vair represented by rows of cup-shaped figures alternately argent and azure (unless other tinctures are specified)

Achievement the complete heraldic display
Addorsed back to back
Alerions usually depicted as eagles without beaks or legs
Annulet a ring, or voided disc or roundel
Armed applied to a beast, refers to its natural weapons, e.g. the claws of a lion
Arms heraldic emblems displayed on a shield or banner; sometimes termed *coat of arms*, or shortly *coat*, from the heraldic surcoat
Attires antlers, or horns

Badge an heraldic device distinct from arms or crest, formerly worn by retainers and, where owned by a college, usable by its members
Banner a rectangular flag on which arms are displayed
Bar horizontal bars across the field, multiple of the fess
Barbed applied to the heraldic rose, refers to the leaf-like sepals appearing between the petals
Barrulet a diminutive of *bar*
Barry divided by three, five or more horizontal lines into an even number of pieces **Barry wavy** having the horizontal lines undulating **Barry wavy argent and azure** frequently represents water
Base the lower part of the shield
Beaked and membered applied to a bird, refers to its beak and legs
Bend a diagonal band from the dexter chief to the sinister base of a shield **In bend** placed diagonally **Per bend** divided by a diagonal line

Bendlet a narrow bend
Bezanty charged with golden roundels
Blazon heraldic description of arms
Bluemantle see Herald
Bordure synonymous with border
Botonny ending in trefoils
Burelly barry of many pieces

Caboshed of a deer's head set full-faced and not including the neck
Cadency exact relationship of the branches of a family to the main line
Caduceus the rod of Mercury, having two wings and entwined by two serpents
Canton a rectangular division in the top dexter corner of the shield
Chapeau an heraldic cap
Charge any object upon the shield or on another object or on a division of the shield
Chevron a figure like an inverted V, the point normally being upwards **Per chevron** divided by a chevronwise line
Chevronel a narrow chevron
Chequy checker-board pattern
Chief the upper part of the shield enclosed by a horizontal line (*chiffe* in early blazon) **In chief** in the upper part
Clarenceux see Heralds
Coat, Coat of Arms see **Arms**
Cockatrice a creature compounded of the head and legs of a cock and the bat-like wings, scaly body and pointed tail of a wyvern
College a corporate foundation, usually established by Royal Charter, complying with University ordinances.
College of Arms, The a corporation of thirteen officers of arms, forming part of the Royal Household, which grants and regulates the use of heraldic insignia and records pedigrees. Its first charter dates from 1484.
Colours the wreath, or torse, forming the base of the crest, and also the mantling, are said to be *of the colours* when they are composed of the first metal and the first colour named in the description of the arms
Compony, or Gobony divided into a series of rectangular pieces of alternating tinctures
Contourny signifying that the whole charge has been reversed to face the sinister
Cotised of a bend enclosed by two narrow bendlets
Couchant crouching, with the head erect

Counterchanged having the tinctures reversed

Couped cut off

Couple-closes narrow chevronels enclosing a chevron

Courant running

Crest an heraldic ornament worn on the helm and (with or without the helm) displayed above the shield

Crest-wreath see **Wreath**

Cross a straight-sided figure extending to the edges of the shield (as in the arms of the University of Cambridge) unless otherwise described. Other forms of cross found in this book are best defined by reference to the illustrations, viz.

Cross botonny fitchy Newnham

Cross flory Girton

Cross formy or paty Selwyn

Cross moline (molen) Regius Prof. of Law

Cross patonce splayed arms and paw-like ends, an early version of the cross flory – St Edmund's

Cross potent Queens'

Cross potent quadrate Selwyn

Cross-crosslet a small cross with each limb crossed

Dancetty deeply indented, or zigzag

Dexter the right hand side from the standpoint of the man behind the shield; consequently the left side to the viewer

Difference an alteration or addition to distinguish arms

Dimidiating combining two shields of arms by figuratively cutting them down the middle and joining the dexter half of one to the sinister half of the other

Displayed describes an eagle having its wings and legs outspread

Doubled lined; see **Mantling**

Embattled having the edge square-notched like battlements

Enarched curved upwards

England short for the royal arms of England: *Gules three lions passant gardant in pale or.*

Engrailed having the edge indented with a series of small curves, points outwards

Ensigned placed immediately above

Enty in base the base of the shield parted per chevron

Eradicated uprooted

Erased torn off, leaving a ragged edge

Escutcheon a shield

Escallop a scallop-shell

Estoile a star with curved rays

Fess or **Fesse** a horizontal band across the middle of the shield

Per fess divided by a horizontal line

Fess point the centre point of the shield

Fesswise (fessways) placed horizontally

Field the ground of the shield   **Of the field** of the same tincture as the ground

First, of the of the same tincture as the one first mentioned in the description of the arms

Fitchée or **Fitchy** pointed at the foot

Fleur de lis a conventional floral form (see Christ's and St John's, King's, Queens') associated with the lily but distinct from the natural lily (see Corpus Christi)

France Ancient short for the old royal arms of France: *Azure semy of fleurs de lis or* **France Modern** the later royal arms: *Azure, three fleurs de lis or*

Fretty interlacing diagonal strips **Fret** a portion of such a design (as in the arms of Magdalene)

Gardant or **Guardant** describes a beast turning its head to face the viewer

Gobony see **Compony**

Gorged encircled about the neck

Goutté d'or sprinkled with gold drops

Griffin an heraldic monster having the head with ears, foreclaws and wings of an eagle, and the body, hind legs and tail of a lion

Gueule See **Gules** among colours

Haurient describes a fish head upwards as though rising to breathe

Helm heraldic helmet

Herald an officer of arms: the chief called kings, the juniors pursuivants. Each has a distinctive name, e.g. Garter King of Arms, Clarenceux King of Arms, York Herald, Bluemantle pursuivant

Impalement combining two coats of arms on one shield by dividing it down the middle and placing one coat in the dexter half and the other in the sinister. The coats are then **impaled**

Indented having the edge serrated with triangular notches

Jessant-de-lis having a fleur de lis 'shooting forth' from it

Label a narrow horizontal strip with a number of pendants, usually three or five, added to arms to denote cadency

Langued tongued

Last, of the of the same tincture as the one last mentioned in the description of the arms

Leopard in early heraldry, synonymous with **lion passant gardant**

Lozenge a figure like the diamond in playing cards **Lozengy** a field of such figures formed by intersecting diagonals, the spaces being of alternating tinctures

Mantling the decorative head-cloth covering the back of the helm and shown falling on each side of the shield. (In this book mantling is shown only in the illustration of the arms of the City of Cambridge. Colleges without crests do not display helms or mantling.) **Mantled** term used when denoting the tinctures of the mantling. These are usually one of the heraldic colours on the outside, doubled, i.e. lined, with a metal or fur

Martlet an imaginary small bird, generally without beak or feet

Mascle a lozenge with a lozenge-shaped perforation

Maunch a lady's sleeve formalized in heraldry

Membered referring to the legs of a bird

Metal see heraldic tinctures above

Mullet (molet) a star-shaped figure with straight rays, five in number unless otherwise stated

Mural crown a crown composed of masonry battlemented at the top

Murally edged like a wall

Nebuly describes a line conventionally representing clouds

Or the metal gold

Orle of denotes the position of a number of objects arranged on the shield so as to follow the line of its edge

Pale a vertical stripe. When two or more appear on one shield they may be termed **pallets In pale** or **palewise** describes objects placed vertically, one above another **Per pale** divided by a vertical line.

Pall a Y shaped form

Party divided. The word is often omitted and understood from such phrases as *party per bend, party per fess* etc.

Passant walking with the right forepaw raised

Patonce see Cross

Pelican in its piety so described when shown feeding its young with blood drawn from its breast

Pheon an arrow head

Plummet a bricklayer's or carpenter's plumb line

Point the lower part of the shield

Pretence, in set on the centre of the shield, to show that the bearer of the main arms pretends to the representation of his wife's family

Proper represented in natural colours

Quadrate see cross

Quarterly the division of a shield into four parts by intersecting vertical and horizontal lines, each such part being termed a **quarter**. When the shield is divided into more than four parts (e.g. Queens') each part is termed a **quartering**

Queued tailed

Rampant rearing erect on the left hind leg

Rayonny streaming with rays

Roundel or **Roundle** a disc

Rousant rising

Sable see tinctures

Saltire a cross placed diagonally **In saltire** or **saltirewise** crossed diagonally

Second, of the of the same tincture as the second one mentioned in the description of the arms

Seeded descriptive of the centre of a rose

Segreant applied to a griffin when rearing on its hind legs with foreclaws raised and wings spread

Sejant sitting

Semé or **Semy** scattered with a number of small objects

Sinister the left hand side from the standpoint of the man behind the shield; consequently the right side to the viewer

Slipped of plants or leaves, tapering at the stem

Supporters human figures or creatures flanking a shield and represented as holding it

Tinctures the metals, colours and furs used in heraldry, listed at the beginning of this glossary

Torse see **Wreath**

Tressure resembles a narrow bordure but not reaching the edges of the shield

Unguled hoofed or having nails or claws

Vair see tinctures

Vert see tinctures

Visitations the periodic visit to the counties of England by officers of arms between 1530 and 1686 to record the lawful arms and the pedigrees of the gentry and the arms of corporate bodies

Vulning 'wounding' usually describes the pelican in the act of pecking her breast to release drops of blood

Volant flying

Wavy describes an undulating line

Wreath, Crest-wreath or **Torse** the twisted material forming the base of a crest. In illustrations six twists are shown, alternately of a metal and colour, which are those predominant in the arms unless otherwise stated

Wyvern resembles a dragon in head, body and wings, but has only two legs

Yale an heraldic monster having a body like an antelope's, a tusked muzzle like a boar's, and horns curving in opposite directions as though capable of being swivelled